D0210987

LEARNING DENIED

LEARNING DENIED

Denny Taylor

With a Foreword by
William L. Wansart

Heinemann
Portsmouth, NH

Heinemann
A division of Reed Elsevier Inc.
361 Hanover Street, Portsmouth, NH 03801-3912
Offices and agents throughout the world

© 1991 by Denny Taylor. All rights reserved. No part of this book may be reproduced in any form or by electronic or mechanical means, including information storage and retrieval systems, without permission in writing from the publisher, except by a reviewer, who may quote brief passages in a review.

Library of Congress Cataloging-in-Publication Data

Taylor, Denny, 1947–
    Learning denied / Denny Taylor : with a foreword by William L. Wansart.
        p.   cm.
    Includes bibliographical references (p.   ).
    ISBN 0-435-08545-X
    1. Special education—United States—Case studies.   2. Exceptional children—United States—Case studies.   3. Learning disabilities—Diagnosis—Case studies.   4. Educational tests and measurements—United States—Case studies.   5. Literacy—United States—Case studies.   I. Title.
LC3981.T38   1990
371.9—dc20   90-44977
                                                                       CIP

Designed by Maria Szmauz.
Front-cover art by Patrick.
Printed in the United States of America.

04 03   DA   14 15

For Patrick
who likes to write stories,
play baseball,
and be with his friends

ltimately, it is intended that this record and analysis be exhaustive, with no detail, however trivial it may seem, left untouched, no relevancy avoided, which lies within the power of remembrance to maintain, of intelligence to perceive, and of the spirit to persist in.

James Agee

Contents

Foreword

hrough all my experiences with people struggling to learn, the one thing that strikes me most is the ease with which we misperceive failed performance.

Mike Rose, *Lives on the Boundary*

In *Learning Denied*, Denny Taylor tells the story of a family's clash with public school, special education bureaucracy. It is a personal story of Claudia and Pat as they attempted first to help their son Patrick in school, and then, ultimately, to protect him from the school. It is also a cautionary tale of educational decision making gone wrong—a tale of reliance on a legalistic decision-making process that allows the participants to forget that there is a real child involved; a tale of a prevailing assessment paradigm that reduces learning to the scores on standardized tests and the cumulative interpretive myth of "experts" who have rarely worked with, or ever tried to teach, the child; where the focus is on what a child is *unable* to do rather than on what the child is *capable* of doing.

Taylor chronicles the school district's pursuit of Patrick's suspected disability. From the early mention of possible perceptual difficulties on a preschool screening assessment to the incessant, and sadly typical, battery of testing throughout his first and second grade years, the school sought to find within Patrick the cause of its own failure. As the intense questioning of his abilities caught up with Patrick, he stopped performing in school. But at home, and during his sessions with Taylor, he read increasingly more difficult books and wrote increasingly more complex stories. As Taylor tells the story we see Patrick's struggle to recognize and demonstrate his literacy contrasted with the school system's response to the specter of perceived problems that virtually denied not only the existence of Patrick's abilities but also, in a certain sense, the existence of Patrick himself.

Some readers may find this family's experience atypical. What is atypical in this story is the fact that the parents resisted the school's attempt to subject their child to relentless testing in an attempt to label him learning disabled before they would teach him. What was unusual is that these parents stopped trusting the school and the tests because they recognized the contradiction between the Patrick they knew and the school's depiction of him, based on test scores, as a student with serious problems. What is commonplace about this family's experience is the attitude about testing that made these events possible.

This story is an example of the reductionistic nature of an assessment process that reduces learning to the scores on standardized tests. It is an example of the popularly held belief that test scores are neutral and objective representations of a student's true abilities, needing no interpretation or regard for the context within which they were derived. While we know that in theory this is not true, in practice the glorification of standardized data over observation prevails. This belief is further coupled with the assumption that the cause of school failure lies within the student. Evaluation, as well as subsequent teaching, are deficit driven. In a reification of the medical model upon which this process is based, the student's school difficulties are reduced to a set of symptoms to be diagnosed. The goal of the diagnosis becomes the delineation of the specific deficits within the student (Poplin 1988).

Standardized tests can, in fact, be helpful in identifying the needs of students who encounter difficulty in school *if* those tests are interpreted carefully, within the context of the whole of the student's experiences. Even more helpful is an analysis of the student's abilities based on an assumption that the student is capable and has learned much that may not be readily apparent. Observations of abilities that contradict test scores should not be denied. Rather, they should be accepted as evidence of the complexity of the student's learning and a challenge to the limitations of standardized tests. Denny Taylor was able to do this with Patrick, and in this book she shows us what he *was* able to accomplish. Similarly, we can learn how to see ability within the behavior of our students, both from this book and from many of Taylor's earlier works, including *Growing Up Literate* (1988) and

"Teaching without Testing" (1990). The school personnel who evaluated Patrick could have also become aware of his abilities. Unfortunately, they chose not to look for them.

I hope that all educators have the opportunity to read this book. Those who engage directly in the testing process need to understand the impact of these invasive procedures from the child's and the family's point of view; *Learning Denied* gives us such a view. Classroom teachers, who refer children for testing with the hope of receiving meaningful educational recommendations, will be equally enlightened.

Parents will be particularly interested in this book. We all need to value parents' right to expect that the school will be an advocate for the abilities of their children, especially if those children experience difficulties in school. *Learning Denied* will also help us examine our expectations for our children's early school experiences as well as our assumptions about failure.

Recently, the mother of a five-year-old boy told me she intended to send her son to a private kindergarten instead of the public kindergarten at their neighborhood school. "I know he has eye–hand coordination problems," she told me. "His eyes have no idea what his hands are doing. I can see it in his art work. But he seems to be doing everything I would expect in reading." Feeling a moment of doubt she added, "He might get more special help in the public school, but they might also label him as learning disabled." Then, with hopeful finality, she concluded, "At the private school he will get an extra year to develop without the school labeling him as having a problem." This parent is concerned about the possibility that the school will "misperceive failed performance." What should we tell her? Is her concern justified? Her son's school story is just beginning. If we heed the lessons of this book, his story may be different. For Patrick, however, the decisions have been made, the files stamped and closed, the story of his early educational experience concluded. But his story lives on in this book. It should not be forgotten.

William L. Wansart
University of New Hampshire

Acknowledgments

his book began as an article for the *Harvard Educational Review* but even printed in twelve-pitch and with the narrowest of margins it was impossible for me to reduce the text to the required length of fifty pages. Nevertheless I am grateful to Judy Diamondstone, who was a board member of the *Harvard Educational Review*, for encouraging me to write. Without her phone calls and *HER* deadlines the book would have taken much longer to write.

There were many times during the four years that are documented in *Learning Denied* that I needed to talk to someone about the events that were taking place in Patrick's young life. On those occasions, I would pick up the telephone and call a friend. Gerald Coles of the Robert Wood Johnson Medical School in New Jersey became what he calls a "telephone buddy." Until I obtained his number through directory inquiries, we had never spoken, and we still haven't met. Nevertheless, we have talked on numerous occasions about Patrick; Gerry examined the documentation that I sent to him; and he wrote a detailed response, excerpts of which are included in *Learning Denied*.

Don Graves of the University of New Hampshire has long been a telephone buddy. When I called about Patrick, Don always made time to listen. I am grateful for the many insights that he provided and for the practical suggestions that he made. William Wansart, also at the University of New Hampshire, talked with me on many occasions about Patrick's literacy learning, and he helped me gain some understanding of the ins and outs of the federal laws and state regulations that govern special education. Bill also agreed to evaluate Patrick, and excerpts of his report of this evaluation are included in the text.

Jerome Harste of Indiana University also listened when I phoned, and he too wrote in response to the documentation that I sent to him. Dorothy Strickland talked with me about Patrick's writing, and on one occasion she constructed an analysis of one of his stories. Gay Su Pinnell, of Ohio State University, discussed Patrick's progress with me on the telephone, and when she saw examples of his writing, she offered to testify on Patrick's behalf at the due process hearing. If the school system had not withdrawn its suit, Don Graves, William Wansart, and Gay Su Pinell would all have attended the hearing.

Special thanks also go to Mary Benton, Debbie Boisvert, Brenda Eaves, Kathy Matthews, and Bruce Turnquist, all dedicated and gifted elementary school teachers, who have offered their support to Patrick and his family during the time in which he has been home schooled. It is impossible for me to overstate the importance of their support, for they provided Claudia and Pat with a tangible link to the educational system that they felt had rejected their son.

Most of all, I want to thank Claudia, Pat, and Patrick, my closest friends. When I began to work with Patrick in February of his first-grade year, I really didn't know his family, other than a wave through a car window or a ''hello'' at the local store. But over the years, as we have worked together our families have gotten to know one another and there have been occasions when Claudia and Pat have helped us through difficult times, as I hope that we have helped them.

Finally, I want to thank my family. David, my husband, has followed Patrick's progress with great interest, and has occasionally enjoyed special times with him, such as a recent visit to a local restaurant to eat pizza and discuss the infinite possibilities created by the launch of the Hubble telescope. Louise and Ben, my children, have also been helpful. School is something they know a lot about. Patrick's struggles came at a time when they were in junior and senior high school, facing struggles of their own. There were times, especially as we were preparing for the due process hearing initiated by the school, when ''How's Patrick doing?'' became a frequent question. From my conversations with Louise and Ben I am sure that their questions were not about whether he could read and write. They had listened to him read, and they had seen him write. I am sure that what they were really asking was how he was coping with the constant questioning of his abilities, for in high school with daily quizzes, followed by midterms and finals, they had both learned how it felt to have one's abilities constantly assessed and reassessed.

As always, and as a postcript here, I want to thank Philippa Stratton, Editor in Chief of Heinemann Educational Books, for providing me with the opportunity to publish this work. At the International Reading Association's annual convention in Atlanta, Philippa thanked her authors and said, ''I honestly don't know how you do it,'' to which I would like to respond, on behalf of all her authors (and, I might add, readers), ''We honestly don't know how you do it, Philippa, but we're all really glad that you do.''

Introduction: Patrick's Solar System

atrick was explaining how Jupiter's recently discovered ring encircles the planet. "When the planet moves it's like thousands, billions, of men are pulling it, trying to get it exactly the same," he said. Then, holding on to an imaginary rope, he mimed the action of the men. Leaning one way and then the other, he said, "When the planet moves, it moves with the planet and it doesn't shift this way when the planet is sitting there. It doesn't shift this way or that way, it just stays in one place, exactly lined up."

It was January 1990, and we were reviewing possible projects to get us started in the new year. Patrick, who was ten years old, wanted to write a book called *Solar System Two*, which he said would expand upon the book on the planets that he had written in the fall. He explained, "In the first book all I did was write down the basic things on the planets—what the temperatures were, how far they were from the sun." Patrick said, "Mostly I think some of the stuff that I have done is just basically the basic stuff on the planets." As we talked, he began to think about the next phase of his Solar System research. "What I'm doing now is finding other information that I don't know about."

The conversation about Jupiter's rings came about as Patrick shared the new information that he had collected since he had finished his first book. He talked about Pluto's elliptical orbit, the tornadoes that create red spots on Jupiter, and the explosions taking place on one of

Neptune's moons. He explained that he hoped to be able to examine the Solar System himself using a friend's telescope. "I might be able to see Venus or something like that. And spots on Venus that I don't know about," he said, anticipating the event. "And—maybe—I don't know—the Moon or Mars or something like that. I *know* I'm going to be able to see Venus because you can see Venus with your naked eye. Right?"

In this way Patrick reorganized the task, recast problem-solving relationships, and generated hypotheses about some of the expected outcomes of his new research project. He theorized about "doing," and as he shared his ideas with me, he demonstrated that he has considerable learner expertise. Patrick himself verified this perspective when he talked about a game of Trivial Pursuit that he had played with his aunts and uncles during the Christmas vacation. He explained that he had asked for questions about the Solar System because he "knew a lot" about it; when they played the game, he said, he was surprised that his relatives didn't know the answers to many of the questions. "Even the hotness of all the planets. It was hard. And the order of the planets. They didn't get them, and I would have thought they *would* get them because to me they seem like easy questions. But they are *really not* easy questions."

Becoming an expert on the Solar System was something that happened to Patrick during the fall of 1989. No one had planned it that way. It was simply one of the perks of his research project. In September, we had used a special edition of *Scientific American*, "Managing Planet Earth," as the basis for the work we did together. One thing led to another, and by the beginning of October we were talking about other planets. Patrick had a large poster of the Solar System, and I suggested that he write a report based upon all the information that he could extract from the pictoral representation. The next time we met, Patrick said that he had decided that the best way to go about the task was to come up with questions. He explained that he had spent a lot of time studying the poster, but it was at odd moments during the day when other things were happening that he had thought of questions that he would like to answer. He said that one question had come to him when he was sitting in the back seat of the car going shopping with his mother. Patrick had written the questions on file cards, and he had numbered them from one to six. He asked:

1. How many moons do each of the planets have?
2. Which planets have rings and what are they made of?
3. How many days or years does it take each planet to go around the sun?
4. Does another planet have life on it?

5. How many planets are there?
6. How cold is the coldest planet, and how hot is the hottest planet?

Patrick had then answered the questions he had generated. The problem he then faced was how to create a report from the information he had gathered. I suggested that we work on it together. "You dictate and I'll write," I said. We had never worked in this way before, so it took a few minutes for us to get started. I wrote "Report on the Solar System" and then "What was your assignment?" Patrick began, hesitantly at first, and with some help from me. But he got the hang of it as soon as he saw how quickly his ideas could be written, exactly as he stated them, on paper. Answering my question about the assignment, he began:

My assignment was to write a report about the Solar System. I studied maps, books, and encyclopedias and newspapers to find information on the planets. I asked myself questions and then what the answers were. I wrote am going to write about every planet . . .

Patrick told me what to cross out and rewrite as he edited the piece, and then, using the information that he had written on the file cards, he started the report. He structured the task so that he began with Mercury, the planet closest to the Sun, and ended with Pluto, which he explained was not always the farthest planet from the Sun because of its elliptical orbit. Patrick spoke quickly, and I hurried to keep up as I wrote exactly what he said. At one point he told me that my writing was getting sloppy, and for a short while he spoke a little more slowly, but his enthusiasm quickly returned us to our original speed, and I found my attention taken with the legibility of my handwriting as I sped across the paper. Occasionally, Patrick would refer back through the pages of text and tell me to add information. After almost two hours of collaboration, we finished what was to become the first of the many drafts that Patrick made of his book on the Solar System. To give you an example of the text, this is what he dictated for the planet Venus:

Venus: Venus has no moons. Venus goes the opposite way than Earth goes. Venus and Earth are sister planets because they are the same size. Venus is the hottest planet because of the "Greenhouse Effect." When you go into a greenhouse it is really hot in there and you have to get out. Venus' temperature is 480 centigrade. It takes Venus 225 days to go around the Sun.

The only planet that Patrick did not include in his report was Earth. He said, "Everybody knows about Earth." However, by the time we met the following week he had added a section on Earth to the draft of his report. He wrote:

Earth: Diameter 7,926 miles. Earth has a moon. Earths surface is made up of land and water. There is more water than land. Earth is the third planet from the sun. The average temperature is 72 degrees F. Earth is the only planet known that has life on it. The atmosphere is 21% oxygen the rest is mostly nitrogen. We need plants to make oxygen. It takes earth one year 365 (check 14?) days to go around the sun.

Patrick had added to the information in his first draft, such as the diameter of each planet, and he had rewritten the report on good-quality drawing paper, arranging the text so that each planet appeared on a separate page. On some pages he had drawn diagrams of the planets, and he had included distinguishing features, such as moons and rings. At this point Patrick had also experimented with the idea of writing the text in script, but quickly abandoned the idea, as he had only just begun to write that way. We talked about the words he was using in his writing, and I asked him if he could make a list of all the technical terms he was learning. By the following week Patrick had added information about the Sun to his report, and he was writing another version using the computer. He showed me the first few pages and said it was getting easier, because his typing was improving as he worked on the report. He had also produced a list of technical terms, entitled "Words in Solar System Report," which included *atmosphere*, *average*, *axis*, *diameter*, and *mantle*. There were lines drawn on the page to indicate which words needed to be moved to place them in alphabetical order.

When we met again later that week, Patrick showed me that he had taken this list and created a glossary for his book. His definitions closely approximated those that he had found in the various books he had been using. However, he had extracted and modified the information to make sense within the context of his own report. For the word *astronomer* he wrote, "A person who knows a great deal about stars and planets by looking at them through a telescope." For *crust* he wrote, "A hard outside part or coating. The crust of the earth is a layer of rock twenty miles deep." And for *temperature* he wrote, "How hot or cold something is. The temperature of the weather or peoples bodies is measured by degrees (with a thermometer)." By this time Patrick had also produced a bar graph, which enabled him to show the distance from each planet to the Sun. He told me that he thought that the diameter of all the planets together would be greater than the diameter of the Sun. So, since he had included the diameter of each planet in his report, we used a calculator to test his hypothesis. Patrick recorded his findings in the section of his report about the Sun. He wrote, "I found that the diameter of the sun (865,318 miles) is bigger than the combined diameter of all the planets (250,213 miles)."

Early in November, Patrick designed several potential covers and chose one that he then used on the final version of his report. On the day that we worked together, Patrick hid the book under the table, and when he eventually showed it to me it was with great ceremony. We looked through the pages together and then he read the entire document to me. We talked about making copies, especially one for his grandfather, and we reflected upon Patrick's own understanding of himself as a learner, for I had asked Patrick the previous week what he had learned about himself as he had worked on the project. Patrick had smiled and, after a moment's hesitation, said, "That I'm smart."

Patrick *is* smart. He finished his Solar System book just a few weeks before he celebrated his tenth birthday. So we can state that at nine years eleven months Patrick could use the social, symbolic, technical, and material resources at his disposal to develop situated explanations of the workings of the Solar System. We can also make some statements about his use of print, for Patrick clearly demonstrated that his personal understandings of literacy are both socially constructed and individually situated in the practical accomplishments of his everyday life. Patrick uses print to:

1. Recast problem–solution relationships.
2. Test hypotheses.
3. Examine contradictions.
4. Change procedural possibilities for problem solving.
5. Create gap-closing solutions.
6. Simplify tasks.
7. Develop flexible problem–solution strategies.
8. Invent new procedures to arrive at instrumental (purposeful) solutions.
9. Lead others in problem solving.
10. Generate new problems.

Perhaps what is most impressive about this list is that it illustrates, paradoxically, that as Patrick used his literacy skills to simplify the research task, the complexity of the project increased. He used print to invent new strategies to generate the information he needed to develop nonroutine problem-solving procedures.

Unfortunately, these demonstrations of learner expertise have not helped him, for the literacy skills that Patrick so ably demonstrates are not the same as the reading and writing skills valued by the school in which he was supposed to receive an education.

By the time this book is published, Patrick will have been denied the right of a public education "to assist students to achieve literacy and to provide the opportunity for each child to learn according to his needs and his abilities" (the state Literacy Instruction and Dropout Prevention Act, 189:54) for more than two years. He works at home with his mother, Claudia, and his father, Pat, both of whom collaborated with Patrick on the Solar System project. Claudia and Patrick talked daily about his research, collaborating in the search for new information and organizing the practical aspects of his daily studies. Pat also played a key role. For example, Pat discussed with Patrick the various forms of the graphs he could use to record the distance from each planet to the Sun, and then he helped Patrick make the bar graph that accompanied his final report. It is in this way that Patrick is becoming literate. The family works hard to provide opportunities for learning that, in their opinion and in mine, the public school has denied.

Remembering the labels that were used to describe Patrick, Claudia said, "It bothers you." She talked "of everything that was wonderful" that was constantly overshadowed by the difficulties that Patrick experienced in school. "I cried a lot," she said with a sad laugh. "I got frustrated, and the frustration came out in tears a couple of times because I just felt like Patrick was never going to be allowed to grow up."

With devastating clarity, Claudia and Pat make visible the personal tragedy of the educational injustices that they have suffered with their young son Patrick since he became "disabled" by the system. Questions were raised about Patrick's learning at the preschool screening, and his abilities were assessed and reassessed through his kindergarten and first-grade years. The repeated testing that was undertaken to discover the medical-genetic or cognitive-psychological "condition" that would enable the school to classify Patrick as an "educationally handicapped" student created the myth of a learning disability that eventually became reified through the school's local interpretation and implementation of federal laws and state regulations.

The situation was aggravated by the conduct of the clinical psychologist who had evaluated Patrick. Recounting what happened as the psychologist came out of his office after a day of testing Patrick, Claudia explained, "He said to me, 'Patrick has learning problems.' " Claudia went on to state that the psychologist was holding Patrick by the hand while he spoke to her. "He wouldn't explain what he meant," she said. "Or how. Or what kind of learning problems he had." Later in the conversation she returned to the evaluation by the psychologist. "I didn't know the results," she said. "Only that he said that Patrick had problems." In her distress, Claudia shared with Patrick's first-grade teacher the comments that had been made by the psychologist at the conclusion of the day of testing. This information became "school knowledge," and the report that the psychologist wrote some four months later became a critical component of the school district's case when legal proceedings were initiated against Claudia and Pat for not acting in the best interests of their son.

Patrick is a bright, articulate child who has been forced to live in the margins of the American educational system. Right from the start his abilities were questioned. There was never a time when the school was willing to acknowledge Patrick's capabilities, or to accept that he could read and write. His learning was (and continues to be) denied. In this book I am asking that we accept societal responsibility for the inappropriate educational decision making that handicapped Patrick by critically damaging his self-esteem and his perception of himself as a learner. I am also asking that we acknowledge the suffering of his parents; and, for his sake as well as theirs, I am asking that we recognize that Patrick is a literate child. I ask this in light of recent research presented in the social science literature that indicates that there are *many* children like Patrick who have been (and continue to be) handicapped by our educational system. Patrick's case is not atypical. Relying on testing to find out what is "wrong" with the child, blaming the child when he or she does not learn in the ways expected in our public institutions, and searching for the glitch in the child's neuro-logical makeup so that the school (system) can be exonerated if and when the child "fails" are all typical of the ways in which we "educate" children. Sapon-Shevin (1989) confirms that Patrick's case is not atypical when she writes:

> Viewing children as deficient leads special education to direct its efforts toward forcing the child to change in order to fit in or be accepted. This approach legitimates behavioral and medical management techniques which attempt to "fix" the child. (92)

Patrick's school experiences are typical. The school tried to make him fit by prescribing medical management techniques to effect a behavioral change (see Taylor 1988; in press). But what is *atypical* is the response of Claudia and Pat to the efforts of the school. They did not believe that their son was disabled, and they refused to cooperate when it was suggested that Patrick be classified as having a language-based learning disability. The school tried to persuade them and eventually to coerce into accepting this label so that Patrick could receive treatment for the problem, according to federally enacted Public Law 94-142.

In their review of "a decade's experience with the implementation of PL94-142" Gartner and Lipsky (1987, 373) focus their attention on the "troubling issues" that lead them to seriously question the accuracy of the labels ascribed to young children. Citing numerous studies, these researchers state:

- More than 80 percent of the student population could be classified as learning disabled by one or more definitions presently in use.
- Based upon the records of those already certified as learning disabled and those not, experienced evaluators could not tell the difference. (373)

Gartner and Lipsky seriously question the tests that are used, and they speak of testing driving the decision-making process. If we add to their position the research of Coles (1978, 1987), which focuses our attention upon the lack of defensible principles in testing practices and procedures, either from a scientific or practical viewpoint, and combine this with the perspective presented by Martin (1988), a kindergarten teacher, we can begin to appreciate the difficulties that Claudia and Pat experienced as they tried to question the accuracy of the label that the school wanted to attach to their son. Martin writes:

Early in the school year, I was asked to meet with school personnel who had administered a screening test to my new kindergarten children during the first weeks of school. To my surprise, test results indicated that fully half of my young students were considered to be "at risk" in one or more crucial developmental areas. One of my brightest students was said to be possibly "learning disabled," and my most skilled artist deficient in fine motor ability. My most cooperative learner was "oppositional" and displayed "negative attitudes." (489)

Martin states that the more she remonstrated and gave counterevidence, the more she was met by "grave, implacable insistence on the validity of the judgments." It is not surprising then that Martin was placed in a confrontational situation similar to that in which Claudia and Pat found themselves. Although Claudia states that she really doesn't "want them for enemies" and argues "that's not what it's all about," by opposing the embedded societal constructions and the school's accepted version of her son's academic status she is fighting "this huge giant" that Pat once described as standing in the way, saying, "No, no, no! You can't do that. That's not the way it's done." Given the socially constructed and culturally defined acceptance of medicalized versions of children's lives, any person, parent or professional, who counters with an alternate perspective is likely to have that perspective denied. We change the child, not the system.

Writing about the decision making of committees of educators, Mehan (1984; see also Mehan, Hertweck, and Meihls 1986) provides confirmation of this position when he argues that:

The purpose of the meeting, indeed the entire referral enterprise, is to solve the student's problem, and to do so by altering or modifying the internal states of the student. (1984, 202)

Mehan argues that technical reports are accepted without question. The system prevails. Mehan states:

Often, different committee members enter committee meetings with views of the student's case and its disposition, e.g., classroom teachers and parents provide accounts of the student's performance that compete with the view of the psychologist or district representative. Yet by the meeting's end, the version of the student's case provided by the psychologist or the district representative prevails. (187)

In March 1988, the school system initiated legal proceedings against Patrick's parents. In preparation for the due-process hearing I wrote a report for Claudia and Pat to present to the hearing officer who had been appointed by the state department of education. However, ten days before the hearing was to take place, Claudia and Pat were told that the lawyer acting on behalf of the school system had withdrawn from the proceedings. The hearing never took place, and the report was never presented. With the permission of Claudia and Pat I have used my report in the construction of this book.

My report presented a review and analysis of all of the records maintained in Patrick's school files. This allowed a detailed chronology of Patrick's schooling as recorded in these documents to be developed. Claudia worked with me on this task, and together we were able to identify and disentangle a number of important events that, in retrospect, appear to reflect the intricate internal decision-making processes that created Patrick's "learning disability." The report is essentially a description of institutional mythmaking at work. In this book I juxtapose the information contained in the document in Patrick's school file with brief descriptions of Patrick's reading and writing as he worked to become a literate child. The descriptions have been constructed from my notes and from the audio recordings that I have made on a weekly basis since I started working with Patrick in February 1987. By that time Patrick was struggling in first grade.

Prekindergarten Developmental Screening: Patrick Is "Identified"

ven before he went to school, Patrick's abilities had been questioned. At the preschool screening in April 1985, Claudia was told Patrick "should be watched" as he might have "possible perceptual problems." Reflecting on that time, Claudia said that the initial screening "got the stuff going," and then she added, "right from the beginning." Looking for potential difficulties, the evaluator watched as Patrick skipped, hopped on his right foot and then his left foot, and bounced a playground ball with both hands. He walked backward, toe to heel, for two meters; ran around three obstacles for a distance of forty-five meters in twelve seconds; and walked forward on the balance board with his eyes focused on a target at eye level. But "problems" were noted when Patrick was told to walk up and down stairs carrying an object in both hands. He did not alternate his feet as he climbed.

In our study of the documentation Claudia asked, "But if they had him carrying something in both hands how would they want him to walk up the stairs and alternate? Would you expect a five-year-old to? They can't —they're taught to hold on to a railing when they go up the stairs. If they're walking upstairs holding something they're not going to have that stability to be able to alternate while they're holding something." Even so, Claudia recalls that it was when the evaluator told her that Patrick did not alternate that she also told her that he might have perceptual problems.

The other "difficulty" that was noted at this time was

that Patrick was "not able to cut on line or to cut out shapes." A triangle was drawn on the document and the note beside it stated "not on line attempt to cut." Below this comment the evaluator had circled "watch for perceptual problem." Half out of the circle there was another note: "maybe lack of practice," and below that note, "Fine Motor planning?" We talked about cutting with scissors and I asked Claudia how much cutting Patrick had done before the screening had taken place. Claudia said, "I told them at the time. I said, 'Patrick does not sit down and do a lot of coloring and cutting and all of that.' I have scissors for him, but I never forced Patrick to do any of that stuff. It was there for him to use if he wanted to, but he never chose to use it." Claudia looked at the record of the screening. "I'm just amazed that they based so much on this," she said. Later, she spoke again about the screening. "He was just a little boy," she said, "who would rather play with balls and trucks, be out in the sandpile, be out in the snow."

Kindergarten: Antigravity Tests and Prereading Readiness

I n September 1985, Patrick entered kindergarten. At that time I was observing in his classroom for a research project in which the researchers had requested observational data from a rural kindergarten classroom. I have a photograph of Patrick at a table working on a book about bears. A mother had cut brown bears out of construction paper, and white paper had been stapled to the bears' stomach. In the photograph Patrick is drawing eyes on his bear. There are five other children at the table. One is watching Patrick as he draws, another is putting eyes on his bear, while another child is holding a red crayon over the white paper as if getting ready to write. Patrick is just one of the group. That's how I remember him. There was nothing unusual about his behavior, and although there were other children in the room who appeared to need extra care and attention, Patrick was not one of them. I can recount only two observations that I made of him. In going through my notes, I found an account of a sharing time in which Patrick talked about his dad's automatic ratchet, which, he explained, his dad put air in and then used to turn screws. The second observation was of Patrick at show and tell. Patrick had brought some acorns to show the other children, and he explained how he had refrigerated them because they needed to be kept at a low temperature before they were planted; otherwise, the acorns would not grow into young oak trees. His teacher suggested that they plant the acorns in flowerpots in the classroom and watch to see if they grew.*

In October 1985, Patrick took the Stanford Early School Achievement Test. The scores that he received gave no indication that Patrick would have difficulties in learning to read and write in school. On the Letters and Sounds subtest his raw score was 20, which placed him at the 94th percentile and at the 8th stanine nationally. Similarly, in the fall conference report, which focused upon "Adjustment to the School Environment," no checks were made in the "Great Difficulty" column. Most checks were in the "No Difficulty" column. His kindergarten teacher wrote:

Patrick has made terrific progress in keeping his hands to himself. He is very interested in the other children—friendly, cooperative—but not always in our activities. Patrick likes to listen to stories, and has had some neat "show and tells."

But by December 2, 1985, questions were being raised. In a report to the administration Patrick's teacher wrote:

- switches hands at midline
- rather clumsy pencil grip
- internal organization seems a problem—doesn't know what to do first—to complete a task
- responds well to routine—has learned appropriate getting-ready activities from repetition
- is impulsive—cuts paper without even looking at it
- needs to be visually focused
- responds positively to assistance (went back and re-did initial poor cutting job when showed how to cut better)
- doesn't ask for help to complete 2 or-more-step tasks
- plods along on own—doing own thing
- quiet, interacts with other children, sometimes in inappropriate ways—wrestling, playfully pushing, squeezing hands of his line partner
- often has trouble finding a willing partner
- usually cooperative in whole group situations
- joins in group discussions, participates in Show @ Tell about 75% of the time
- has appropriate level of gross motor skills for a kindergartner. [Physical education instructor] will directly report on his observations in P.E.

---

* Claudia recently commented that she still occasionally finds plastic bags filled with acorns in the refrigerator.

- following directions is a problem
- had trouble with auditory sequencing activity also auditory discrimination activity.

The note from the physical education teacher addressed the director of special education directly and stated, "It appears that Patrick may need to improve his gross motor skills but that this development will come with more exposure to activity." This document is also dated December 2, 1985.

On December 9, 1985, a referral was written by Patrick's teacher. The reasons given were as follows:

Patrick has difficulty following directions. When a task is explained to the group, Patrick often does something quite different. Drawing and cutting skills are less developed than those of most 5/6 year olds. Patrick switches hands at midline.

A conference was arranged with Claudia and Pat, who were worried about the meaning of the referral. Thinking back to that time, Claudia said, "I remember wanting to be aware if there was a problem. They were the experts, and we wanted to know. We just weren't the kind of people to say there's nothing wrong with my child." In the summary of that meeting, the resource room teacher wrote:

To further understand and be able to address Patricks needs we feel that an occupational therapy evaluation is required. The results of this evaluation will help us answer your questions/concerns you have raised regarding Patrick.

Thus the questions raised by the school became "family questions," and Claudia and Pat became a part of the referral process that was initiated. Early in January 1986, Claudia and Pat were given a "Parental Permission for Assessment" form. The means of assessment were described as follows:

A Formal Classroom Observation then individual achievement testing in the Areas of Reading @ Math Woodcock-Johnson test of Achievement for Reading Key Math for math achievement for math [sic].

The reasons given for the assessment were:

In order to contribute to the process of determining whether an educationally handicapping condition exists.

Pat signed the document, giving his permission for the assessment, on January 13, 1986; however, arrangements were not made for Patrick to take these tests until he was in first grade.

On January 31, 1986, Patrick's teacher wrote on his progress report:

Patrick is making progress in his pre-reading and math skills. We are encouraging more verbal interaction in the group and continuing to work on letters and sounds and auditory discrimination.

In the "No Difficulty" box on the progress report, checks were entered for the following "accomplishments":

Shows concentration in group activities
Shares with others and takes turns
Is developing self-confidence
Listens to directions
Participates willingly in group activities
Remembers school rules
Plans own activities
Shows concentration in individual activities
Works without disturbing others
Finishes work in reasonable time
Respects property
Listens without interrupting
Recognizes some alphabet: capital
Knows left to right progression
Identifies common sounds
Knows colors
Can see likenesses in objects, pictures, letters
Can see differences in objects, pictures, letters
Simple number concepts
Count objects

"Some Difficulty" was noted with checks for:

Knows directions in space
Can balance
Can hop and skip
Can cut
Can trace and outline
Follow directions
Participate willingly in discussions
Speaks clearly and fluently
Recognizes some beginning sounds
Hears likenesses and differences in sounds
Identifies rhyme
Geometric figures
Recognizes some numerals

"Great Difficulty" was noted in the following areas:

Knows body parts
Can copy design

Sometime in the spring of 1986, Patrick was observed in his classroom by the resource room teacher. The report of this observation was never sent to Claudia and Pat. Claudia discovered it in Patrick's file at the time of the due process hearing. In our analysis of the records, Claudia and I had become concerned about the number of contradictory statements made about Patrick during his kindergarten year. The report of this particular observation added to our concern, and we began to sense that there was no consistency in the internal workings of the system. For example, one comment—"Appeared to take some of his ideas from other students"—we reread later in light of further written comments that were made about Patrick during his kindergarten year. On some notes, written in May 1986, that Claudia found in Patrick's file, the following comment was made: "Does not take cues from other students and teacher in class. Immaturity?" Statements such as this confirmed for us that Patrick's files were filled with contradictory observations that created an invalid and misleading record of learning disabilities.

At the recommendation of a friend, Claudia and Pat decided to "put an end" to all the questions that had been raised by the school system. They arranged for Patrick to be evaluated using the Gesell Developmental Evaluation. The results of this test, which was administered on March 12, 1986, were "mixed." In the "final thumb-nail summary of behavior" it was stated that Patrick was:

eager and cooperative; intellectually curious; sits well, sustains well; good verbal skills; minimal responses; occasional language reversals; needs time to deliberate and respond, to explore, experiment and finish.

The report also noted "some atypical behavior responses," and it stated that "he has difficulty with right-left orientation and directionality." It is interesting to note that the examiner wrote in the report that "Patrick shows real strength in visual processing skills (7 yrs.)." In an accompanying letter to Claudia the examiner states, "I've included copies of the Visual Memory Subtest. He really did do well with it, wanting more than the 10 that is allowed for each card (like an older child!)". This statement was later contradicted when the school administered a second Gesell in June 1986. Following this administration of the test (by another examiner), it was stated, "It should perhaps be noted that the two areas where Patrick had the most difficulty (steps 6 and 10 of the Cube Test of Visual 3) both require visual memory.'' This time Patrick's age, based on the designs, was given as 4.5–5. These contradictory statements were made based upon the Visual 3 responses made by Patrick in March and June 1986 (see Figure 1).

On March 18, 1986, six days after the first administration of the Gesell, Patrick was evaluated by an occupational therapist. On the way to the hospital where the evaluation was conducted Patrick complained of a headache, and he told his mother that he did not feel well. Claudia talked to the occupational therapist and suggested that they postpone the evaluation. The therapist said she thought that they should go ahead and reassured Claudia by promising to stop the testing if she thought Patrick was too sick to continue. On the report of the testing the evaluator wrote:

Patrick apparently had a temperature and sore throat during the test situation and his performance needs to take this into account. He was obviously not at his best. However, even at maximum performance, some observations were made that are indicative of his usual style.

Although this last statement is confusing and difficult to interpret, the list of tests is not:

Southern California Sensory Integration Tests
Subtests: Visual Form and Space Perception

Space Visualization
Figure-ground Perception
Position in Space
Design Copying

Subtests: Tactile-Motor Perception
Kinesthesia
Manual Form Perception
Finger Identification
Graphesthesia
Localization of Tactile Stimuli
Double Tactile Stimuli

Postural and Bilateral Coordination (Listed as ''skills,'' not subtests)
Ocular-Motor Control
Rapid Forearm Movements
Postural Insecurity
Equilibrium Reactions
Anti-gravity Positions
Hopping, Skipping, Jumping

Figure 1 Patrick's Visual 3 Responses. A: March 1986 (Age Six Years, Three Months). B: June 1986 (Age Six Years, Six Months).

Ball Handling Skills
Crossing the Midline

Goodenough Draw-a-Person Test

Despite the statements in the evaluation report about taking into consideration the possible effects of Patrick's being sick, this is not reflected in the body of the report. The evaluator states:

Although attention span was good on a one-on-one basis, it was felt that Patrick had difficulty in going from one task to the next and needed cuing for each one. During the tests, he exhibited a lot of kicking and slid down in his seat frequently. Patrick was difficult to position, especially during the tactile tests and needed to be re-position [*sic*] and placed again. As we continued the tactile tests, he became itchy, wiggly and at one point stopped breathing as he concentrated.

The four Visual Form and Space Perception tests were conducted to "assess how the brain processes information from the eyes and how the brain rotates visual images and spatial images." Based upon these tests, the evaluator stated, "I feel concern that he [Patrick] may encounter difficulties as he progresses to higher level academics."

The six Tactile-Motor Perception tests were administered to assess "how the brain is able to process the information that comes from the skin and joint receptors to allow for interpretation of touch and movement." It was noted that Patrick "was able to look at a motor movement and imitate it but slowly."

The Postural and Bilateral Coordination part of the evaluation was conducted to assess "how the two parts of the body coordinate, how the two hemispheres of the brain communicate with each other and balance." It is then noted in the report that "how effectively the body is able to make postural adjustments and assume anti-gravity positions is a necessary pre-requisite for basics needed in writing, reading, and other academics."

Patrick's ocular control was also assessed in this series of tests. His "rapid forearm movements" were examined, and he was tested for "postural insecurity" and "equilibrium reactions." Problems were noted when Patrick "was unable to assume various anti-gravity postures without great exertion." The evaluator states in the report that "some residual primitive or infant reflexes were also seen, which would interfere with good balance." In our review of this report, Claudia spoke of the conversation she had had with the evaluator, who had told her on the day of the testing of the findings of the antigravity testing. Claudia said, "I remember telling her that Patrick was riding a bicycle without training wheels when he was four years old. How could he have problems with balance?'' Claudia said she was told that was ''different.'' Reflecting on this, Claudia commented that of course it was different. The occupational therapist had Patrick lie on the floor on his stomach and raise his arms and legs in the air and hold them up for as long as he could.

Hopping, skipping, and jumping were also assessed, and the evaluator noted that Patrick ''performed with heavy tread, as though needing extra sensory input.''* It was noted for ball handling that Patrick ''has some difficulty with catching, possibly due to his visual-motor skills.''

In the summary the therapist stated:

Patrick was a delight to test except that he wasn't feeling well and this might have influenced his scores to some extent. It is felt, however, that most of the results are valid and are indicative of the difficulties that he is having in the classroom.

After the tests were completed, Claudia took Patrick to the family doctor. Patrick had a strep throat and a high temperature. Claudia and Pat expressed their concern about this occupational evaluation becoming a part of Patrick's permanent record. However, although sections of the evaluation were later readministered, the original report remained in his file and was referred to both in subsequent reports and in meetings. On one undated note it was stated, ''Father concerned because Patrick sick on day of test. [Therapist's name] realizes this—still feels tests were rela. acc. will admin other tests if requested—or the same if nec.''

On April 16, 1986, Claudia took Patrick to the optician, as there had been a question raised in the occupational therapy evaluation about some ''ocular-motor irregularity.'' No ocular dysfunction was found during the examination.

In the Spring Conference Report there were no checks in the ''Great Difficulty'' column, and the kindergarten teacher wrote:

Patrick is quiet and cooperative in the classroom, although he sometimes forgets the rules on the playground. His attention span has lengthened appropriately this term. We have some concerns regarding Patrick's pre-reading readiness and are awaiting the results of the O.T. testing.

Patrick took the Stanford Early School Achievement test at about this time, and again his scores were well within the accepted range. On

---

* Patrick is a skilled baseball player. When he was nine he was chosen for the All Stars team for Little League. When he was ten he was chosen for the majors. He won a triathlon race when he was nine, plays soccer and basketball, and skis downhill with considerable expertise.

the Letters and Sounds test he had a raw score of 26, while the average raw score for the 63 students at his grade level was 24.52. This score placed him in the 86th percentile nationally. On the Aural Comprehension test his raw score was 22, while the grade average was 23.01. Nationally, he placed in the 66th percentile. Patrick's combined raw score total for all of the tests was 109, while the average combined score for the 63 students in his grade was 107.11. Patrick placed in the 84th percentile nationally.

The summary of the staffing meeting held on May 13, 1986, notes, "Seems 'gap' between Patrick and other age peers is widening. Is very hesitant, doesn't take risks or sequence activities very well." The occupational therapy test is mentioned, and it is noted that the occupational therapist took into consideration that Patrick was sick at the time of testing. It is then stated that, "Visual form: 4 sub-tests show at *least* -1.0 = dysfunction. Tactile-motor perception: 4 of 6 sub-tests below where you would want." Similar statements continue, and the summary concludes with recommendations for "LD testing for sequencing particularly w/[doctor's name], OT, classroom modification, motor practice at home." Under "further information" it is again stated that the doctor who specializes in the treatment of LD children should examine Patrick. It is also recommended that the tactile portions of the OT be readministered and that "speech-language testing for auditory functioning" be given.

Claudia and Pat attended this staffing meeting and signed the summary. Alarmed at the possibility that Patrick had some kind of disability that they had never noticed, Claudia raised the question of dyslexia. She explained to the school team that the person who had administered the first Gesell had suggested that Patrick might be dyslexic. Claudia's statements became a part of the record. It was noted that the OT evaluator thought it was more likely to be "visual perceptual problems," but the possibility that it might be dyslexia was incorporated into the written record, and so became a part of the "shared knowledge" of the special educators and teachers who were evaluating Patrick. In retrospect, Pat remembers that it was at this time that he told the school that he had a niece (now at college) who was thought to have been dyslexic. This information also became incorporated into the school record.

On May 15, 1986, a speech-language evaluation was conducted. It was noted in the evaluation report that the occupational therapy evaluation had "revealed possible visual perceptual difficulties." The speech-language pathologist conducted an oral motor examination. He noted a "slight space between his upper front teeth" but stated that Patrick's "oral-motor structures were found intact." The Clinical Evaluation of Language Functions (CELF) was administered. This test consists of eleven subtests divided into Processing and Production sections. In the Processing section, Patrick "passed all six subtests above age-expected grade level criteria." His combined score "placed him in the 55th percentile for kindergarten and 30th percentile for grade one." On the Production section, Patrick passed three of the five subtests. His score "placed him in the 45th percentile for kindergarten and the 30th percentile for grade one." It is noted by the pathologist that Patrick had particular difficulty with the Confrontation Naming subtest. This test requires the child "to name 36 items by color and shape within 120 seconds." The pathologist states, "Patrick identified 18 items correctly. Errors were made when Patrick named circles as "O's" and triangles as rectangles. This was not consistent, in that Patrick did correctly identify items such as circles and triangles on the same lines as errors." It is then noted that "if Patrick had not made these errors his language age would have been 6 years and 4 months." The pathologist went on to administer the Expressive One-Word Picture Vocabulary Test. Patrick received an age level of six years, eleven months on this test. Since Patrick was six years, six months at the time of testing, this placed him in the 58th percentile for his age.

Based upon these tests, the pathologist made the following recommendations:

In terms of vocabulary, Patrick needs to be more expressive in describing items, focusing on meaning. These skills can be worked on with a speech pathologist or a resource room teacher. At this time I recommend a speech pathologist for a trial period, to ensure other language skills are not affected and to develop ideas for both the resource room and regular class room teacher.

Just six days after this speech-language evaluation, Patrick began a week of testing at school. From May 21 to May 26, 1986, the Murphy-Durrell Reading Readiness Analysis was administered. Patrick's scores on these tests were as follows:

Test	Maximum Possible Score	Score	Percentile	Stanine
Phonemes (Part 1)	20	19		
Phonemes (Part 2)	28	25		
Total	48	44	80	7
Letter Names (Part 1)	26	23	62	6
Letter Names (Part 2)	26	25	94	8
Total	52	48	84	7
Learning Rate	18	16	92	8
Total Test	118	108	89	8

On July 14, 1986, another staffing meeting took place, with the director of special services attending the meeting. Noted in the summary of that meeting, in the section headed "academic findings," is that on the Spring Stanford Early School Achievement Test Patrick "improved in all sections." The administration of the Murphy-Durrell Reading Readiness test is also noted, but Patrick's scores are not included. Instead the document focuses upon the speech-language evaluation. The Processing section, on which Patrick "passed all six subtests above age-expected grade level criteria," is noted and dismissed in a sentence, and the remaining comments focus upon the Production section of the CELF. The staffing summary states that:

Patrick was nervous, concerned with how well he did—minimal eye contact. Patrick is very quick to respond—this may have compounded things. Some difficulty with sequencing. Patrick's scores on the C.E.L.F. tended to fluctuate. [Name of speech pathologist] feels this is characteristic of children with language processing difficulty.

Claudia and I reread the evaluation report several times, but we were unable to find any basis for this last statement, which directly contradicts the results of the Processing subtests administered to Patrick. We can only presume that the statement was made based upon a conversation between the director of special services and the speech pathologist who administered the test. In any event, however the information was obtained, it was used as the basis for a recommendation by the school that Patrick be examined by an audiologist.

On Patrick's final kindergarten progress report in June 1986, there were no checks in the "Great Difficulty" column. "Some Difficulty" continued to be noted for hopping and skipping and following directions, but most checks were in the "No Difficulty" column. The kindergarten teacher wrote:

Patrick's language development has grown this last term as have his interactions with his peers. He is so cooperative and helpful! Patrick is a very bright little boy, and we agree that he needs the extra time of another year in kindergarten. I am looking forward to the opportunity of working with Patrick again.

When Claudia reread this statement she said sharply, "We didn't agree! I signed this to let them know I had read it, not because I agreed that Patrick should stay in kindergarten."

Claudia and Pat refused to give their permission for the school to retain Patrick in kindergarten.

Summer 1986:
"Resistance to
Being Touched
with Eyes Closed"

n June 25, 1986, a second Gesell test was administered, this time by the school and as noted earlier, the results presented a different interpretation of Patrick's development than the Gesell administered three months previously.

Patrick was evaluated by a certified clinical audiologist on July 31, 1986. No problems were found. The audiologist ended the letter about the evaluation by stating:

I explained the test results to Patrick's mother and she asked about perceptual problems. I explained further that my testing indicates that peripherally his hearing is fine, however, I cannot vouch for what happens to the sound once it reaches his brain.

On August 21, 1986, the occupational therapist conducted a re-evaluation, readministering six tests. The therapist noted a slight improvement but stated:

Still seen today was some resistance to being touched and positioned with eyes closed. At times, Patrick's attention for the task was at risk and I had to bring him back to task. If these tests had been a full battery, he would have been much more fatigued.

Following a meeting with Claudia and Pat, the school agreed to place Patrick in grade one "on a trial basis." In a letter to Claudia and Pat the elementary counselor states, "The trial will be for the first six weeks of school. After the trial period, we will schedule a conference to discuss Patrick's progress."

Claudia and Pat spent much of the summer watching Patrick and watching each other. They asked themselves, "What are we doing wrong? Why is all this happening?" Patrick rode his bicycle, played ball, swam. He was agile, healthy, athletic. He had friends over, and he played with his cousins. Pat and Claudia listened to Patrick as he talked and, as they had always been, they were fascinated by the questions that he asked. Claudia remembers Patrick asking her, "Where do our voices go when we talk?" "I asked him," Claudia said, " 'What do you mean?' " "Well, the noise," Patrick answered. "Where does it go?" Claudia chuckled, remembering. "We had a conversation," she said, "about whether our voices are still out there and we just can't hear them." The moment passed. Claudia was remembering that summer. "We felt so miserable," she said. "It's hard remembering. The other stuff overpowers the good things that happened. The terrible times creep in, and I can't remember the happy times."

Looking back, Pat said it was "very rough." Claudia explained, "It's hard to know whether you're doing the right thing—whether you're just looking for something that really isn't there, and seeing something that really isn't there. Or whether you're right on and they're a little off. It's really hard." It was during that summer that they came to appreciate that the child that they observed at home did not fit with the reports that they read of the child in school. Patrick was lost in the nit-picking reports that were written by "experts" who only saw him in testing situations. "As I read the documents," Claudia explained, "what really bothered me was that none of the examiners knew Patrick. They didn't know how excited he was when he first went to school or how much he wanted to learn to read."

Thinking back to that time, Pat remembered how the decision was made to have Patrick evaluated by a clinical psychologist:

It's a logical sequence, you know, and you're just taught, well, that's how things are done. You know, you test the kid and find out you got a problem. You've got to do this and that and test some more, and I guess we've just gone on and we've taken it one step further. After we were told about this person by the woman who gave us the first Gesell, you know, she mentioned his name. And so we figured, "Well, we'll get right to the bottom of this thing right now at the beginning of the year. We won't mess around." At that point, when that happened in September we had already been through that summer with the occupational therapy tests and this, that, and the other thing, and it seemed to us that the school was just really sloppy about the way they were handling things.

Claudia and Pat made an appointment for a clinical psychologist to evaluate Patrick. The date was set for the third week in September.

First Grade: Therapy on an Individualized Basis

 n the meantime, Patrick was on trial in first grade, and Claudia and Pat were on trial with him. It had been their decision to place Patrick in first grade. If he failed, they would fail with him. At nine o'clock on Monday mornings, as the children in his classroom were getting organized for a morning of reading and writing activities, Patrick left the room to work with the speech-language pathologist. In a report written in February the pathologist wrote:

Patrick is doing well thus far. After an initial adjustment period during which it was difficult to hear him. Except for occaisional [*sic*] refusals Patrick completes assigned tasks.

Twice a week, when Patrick arrived at school, he worked with the pathologist in what is referred to as "therapy on an individualized basis." On two other mornings each week, Patrick worked with an occupational therapist. The stated goals of these therapy sessions were to increase gross motor skills, to increase fine motor skills to enhance classroom performance, and to increase sensory processing. The therapist stated:

Therapy emphasis has been on allowing Patrick experiences which encourage the use of both sides of his body in co-ordinated efforts to enhance gross and fine motor skills.

Thus, while Patrick practiced these "skills" outside of the classroom, the other children in his class were learning to read and write inside the classroom.

On September 15, 1986, Patrick was evaluated by the clinical psychologist. The testing lasted all day, except for a break both in the morning and in the afternoon, when the psychologist took Patrick to a local store and bought him an ice cream and some candy, and a lunch break, which Patrick spent with Claudia. The psychologist administered the following tests:

- Wechsler Intelligence Scale for Children—Revised
- Clinical Evaluation of Language Function
- Beery VMI
- Wide Range Achievement Test
- Personality Inventory for Children
- Peabody Picture Vocabulary
- Lateral Dominance Examination
- Asphasia Screen
- Sensory and Perceptual Exam
- Trail Tests
- ABC Test for Ocular Dominance*

In the first week of October 1986, Patrick took the California Achievement Test with the rest of the children in his classroom. The tests were administered over a period of five days. The results of these tests would eventually be used by the school to support the contention that Patrick was a learning disabled child.

Patrick found it difficult to complete the reading and writing activities that he missed while he was attending the prescribed therapy sessions, and he was constantly trying to catch up with the other children. No mention is made of these difficulties in Patrick's first quarter progress report. He received a "Satisfactory" for "Listens to and follows directions," and his teacher wrote: "Patrick has had a good beginning. He tries so hard to please. His skills are developing."

Claudia talks of the changes she observed in Patrick at this time. He did not want to go to school and was easily upset at home. At the beginning of the year he worked with a small group of children in learning to read using Distar. He copied sentences from the board:

Tim is in the pit.
Tim hid in it.
The fat pig ran to the pit.

---

* Patrick remembers this day of testing. In August 1989, he visited the town where the clinical psychologist used to have his office. Looking around, Patrick commented to his dad, "I remember this place. I had to come here and stay for two days."

Dot and Tom ran to Al.
Tom is not mad at Al.
Dot is not mad at Al.
Is Al bad?

The jet did not hit the man.
The man is mad at the jet!
Can Bob get his jet?

He was given a spelling list on Monday and a spelling test on Friday. He had a phonics workbook in which he worked on a daily basis, and another series of dittos called "See and Do." In addition, Patrick had a math workbook in which he practiced addition and subtraction.

The results of the California Achievement Test were received early in October, and on October 12, 1986, some notes were written that Claudia found in Patrick's file in April 1988, as she was preparing for the due process hearing. In these notes it is stated that Patrick's "attention span seems to be fine." It is noted that the "greatest problem —writing paper—copying from the board." At the bottom of the page the writer states, "last few weeks not wanting to come to school—strep throat."

Patrick complained of stomachaches and was often sick. He told Claudia that the older kids on the bus teased him; she spoke to his first-grade teacher about the situation. In some further notes that Claudia found in Patrick's school file it states: "Beginning of frust. and school avoidance." At the bottom of the page the writer states, "Problems on Sch. Bus. Would not stay in his seat—refused to get on the bus. Kids were not picking on him until he *made himself* different" (emphasis added).*

At a staffing meeting on October 22, 1986, Claudia and Pat met with the first-grade teacher and the elementary counselor. Claudia says that it was at that time that Patrick's teacher said she couldn't help him. "I remember," Claudia said, "she said, 'I don't know what to do for him. I can't help him.' "

Patrick was told that he did not have to copy from the board and he did not have to alphabetize his spelling words. He was removed from his reading group that had advanced to the Holt preprimers, and he was placed back in Distar on his own.

In January 1987, Pat telephoned the clinical psychologist and asked

---

* When Claudia read the manuscript for this book she said, "I called the bus drivers and asked them if they had had a problem with Patrick, and they said they'd never had any problems with Patrick on the bus."

for the report of the September 1986 evaluation. After several phone calls, Pat made an appointment to see the psychologist and collect the report. When he and Claudia arrived on January 23, 1987, the psychologist was sitting at his computer, still writing the report. Pat says they had to wait about thirty minutes for him to finish. Under "Impression" the psychologist wrote:

1. Developmental Dyslexia
2. Attention Deficit Disorder
3. Developmental Language Disorder

Claudia and Pat were no longer able to cope with the situation. They saw no point to further testing. Patrick had taken enough tests. The information they had gained from the tests did not help them understand what was happening to him. Disillusioned with the opinions of the "experts," Pat and Claudia decided to educate themselves. They went to the library at a nearby college and searched the shelves for books on learning disabilities. They spoke on the telephone with the authors of a linguistic reading program that was recommended by the clinical psychologist, and they had literature describing the program sent to their home. They also spoke with a consultant from the Bureau of Instruction for Elementary and Secondary Educational Services who listened to them as they described what had happened to Patrick in school. The consultant told them that she would speak to the Superintendent of Schools for the district—"to make him aware of the parents' interactions with the director of special services and their concerns." Later, the consultant stated that the superintendent's response was noncommittal.

On his second quarter progress report Patrick received a "Satisfactory" in most categories, including "Works well with others" and "Listens and follows directions." His first-grade teacher commented:

Patrick tries hard to please, but finds the work difficult. It is important that we complete his testing process.

In February 1987, Don Graves asked me to write a theoretical paper on assessment from an ethnographic point of view for the National Council of Research in English. To accomplish this task, I began working with two children, one of whom was Patrick. The theoretical paper was eventually published (Taylor 1988); I continued to work with Patrick.

In that February of Patrick's first-grade year, the director of special education was recommending a re-evaluation, which meant more tests would be administered to find the ''glitch'' that was interfering with the ways in which Patrick was learning in school. Claudia and Pat asked if it would be possible for me to do an alternate evaluation, and the director of special education agreed.

On February 16, 1987, Patrick visited me for the first time. We talked about reading and writing. He brought some of his favorite books from home, and we looked at them together. In a small voice Patrick talked about the books his mom and dad read to him.

''I have tons of books,'' he said.

''Does your Mom read them to you?''

''Yeah. Upstairs in my room there's one bookshelf and another bookshelf in my room. Two bookshelves in my room and another bookshelf for Elizabeth. . . . Then downstairs we have another one.''

''That's a lot of books.''

''But the ones upstairs I use for reading.''

We looked at some of Patrick's schoolwork. We talked about the writing that he copied from the chalkboard, and then we looked at a workbook page.

''Guess what I did? This is in my reading book.''

''This is in your reading book?''

''Yep.''

On the paper were animals, a pig jumping rope, a cow riding a bicycle. Patrick led me through the exercise.

''What did you have to do?''

''Circle the ones that really couldn't happen and really could happen.''

''Oh, I see.''

''So. Could a horse really run?''

''Err. Yep.''

''Could a pig really jump rope?''

''Mmm. Not really, I don't think. Is that right?''

''Yep. Could a bear get in jail?''

''Mmm. Probably. Well. He couldn't get in jail, but he might be behind bars in a zoo. But he wouldn't be in jail, would he?''

''Right.''

We finished the exercise, and Patrick then showed me how to do a phonics workbook page. Then I encouraged him to write a story.

''I'm going to write a short story.''

''Okay.''

Patrick proceeded to write the story shown in Figure 2.

'' 'Once I was in—on—' Okay. 'Once I was on a—' How do you spell *mountain*?''

Figure 2   Patrick's Mountain Story

wus   I wus①n
a mountain
then I put mi
Stes on I Sked doono
the mountain
then I clat n then
I gotup and I strad
Skendooon the mountain
the I so a prsin,
and it wus midd and mom
and a I si+r

"I'll write it down for you if you like. This is a long word you're writing."

Patrick chuckles, and copies the word *mountain*.

"Terrific. 'Once I was on a mountain.' "

Patrick continues to write.

" 'The—then.' Very good," I say.

Patrick writes. He points to a word I had written earlier, when we were talking about skiing. "What's that say?" he asks.

"This is skiing. What do you need?"

Patrick writes. He sounds out. "What's this say?" he asks.

"You're spelling *down*?" I say. "Okay. I can read it. 'Once I was on a mountain. Then I put my skis on. I skied down.' Right. And you made it a very long *down*, as if it is a long mountain and you're going down it. That's fine. And 'I skied down.' Terrific. What happened?" (Figure 2 shows the rest of the story.)

Patrick's second story began:

Once upon a time there was a frog that lived in a log. It was a clean log. Then suddenly there was a dark shadow. It was

At this point Patrick stopped and edited his story. He wrote "He was scared." "Can you read that?" he asked before continuing his story:

He was scared. It was just a tree. "Today I am going to pack up and I am going to climb a mountain. A rocky side," the frog said. It was hard to climb the mountain. Then the frog fell. He went over the cliff. But he was on a safe mountain. Then he fell in the lake. He was mad.

In the weeks that followed Patrick wrote many stories. He would write and I would read. At these times we would talk about writing. On one occasion I added a story line to *Frog, Where Are You?* by Mercer Mayer. The story began, "This is Patrick, his puppy and his frog."

"Why do we write puppy—How do you—Why do you write p-u-p-p-y?" he asked.

"Because that's puppy. If you want—"

"Sounds like [Patrick sounds out in a whisper] puh-uh-p-puh-uh-p."

"To there it's *pup* and the extra p-y make *pee*."

"It sounds like an *e*."

"It sounds like an *e* but there isn't an *e*. There the *y* makes the *e* sound."

"Oh" (almost groaning).

"Like the end of *happy*. *Happy* has a *y* at the end that says *e*. Sometimes *y*'s do say *e*'s."

In the next story Patrick wrote, he remembered spelling *puppy* p-u-p-p-y. He also remembered the story that he had written during his previous visit to my house. This story became a variation, another version of his mountain story, and he included the puppy that he had read in the story that I wrote for him.

I like to climb mountains. It is scary. I am climbing [name of mountain] tomorrow. I fell down the mountain today. I fell in the lake. I was mad, just like the frog. Then the frog climbed the mountain. He fell too. We are mad. We got out. The puppy fell too. The puppy growled. We were all mad. Even the puppy was mad.

It is important to note that at the time that Patrick was constructing these stories out of school, he was still being removed from his classroom in school to attend occupational therapy and speech and language services.

On February 6, 1987, the speech-language pathologist wrote:

Story completion is being worked on through sentence completion at this time. Given a visual cue (picture) he can complete the sentence.

Among the workbook pages and dittos that comprise most of Patrick's work in first grade, there are a few stories that he wrote on the backs of pages copied from a Disneyland coloring book. Claudia explained that these were stories that Patrick occasionally wrote when his other work was completed. On the back of a picture of a Disney mouse who has knocked over a pot of honey Patrick wrote:

"Mickey Mouse have you been in the honey?"
"Yes Mom."
"Why did you get in the honey?"
"Because I [needed] some to eat."
"You know you are not allowed to get into the honey."
"I know, Mom."
"Well why did you get into the honey?"
"Because I told you once. I wanted some."
"Well you get some after dinner."
                        The end.

Among Patrick's work were several other stories. These were written following an idea given at the beginning of a sentence. One of these dittos began, "The worst part about having a talking dog is . . ." Patrick wrote:

. . . that he always talks and when I try to get to sleep he says to me, "can I have a book?" And I say, "read quick." And guess what? He does. He reads loud. "I can't get to sleep," I say. This morning he tried to make a milkshake. But he kept the cover off. He pressed blend when the cover was off everything went all over the place. But I say, "love my dog."

There were smiling faces drawn by Patrick's first-grade teacher on the Disney pictures that he colored, but no comments were made on the texts Patrick had written on the other side of the paper. This was not surprising, for in Patrick's first-grade classroom most of the writing was done to complete workbook pages and to fulfill basal curriculum requirements. His teacher was not trained in process writing, so these stories, in which Patrick reinvented the patterns of traditional orthography, were not counted in the evaluative process.*

On February 25, 1987, a meeting was held that I was allowed to attend. In the director of special education's notes, Patrick's teacher is quoted as stating at the beginning of the meeting that she "saw at the beginning of the year a happy bouncy boy—now unhappy." A summary is also included of Patrick's story writing and what it told us about his ability to construct written language. The director of special education wrote, "Patrick is actively trying to construct written language for himself." He then writes, "I mentioned the long term effect of 1 on 1—i.e. inability to work as a member of a group." The notes end:

The issue of coding and special education—i.e. the need to complete the evaluation of speech & OT resources are to be continued. Mr. and Mrs. ———— would like to suspend the special education evaluation process. Patrick will be re-referred if the need arises.

It was agreed that Patrick would not be removed from his classroom for special services and that his teacher would work with him to help him understand the organization of the activities that usually took place while he was out of the room. It was also agreed that he would read in the same basal series as the rest of the children and that I would work with him at home to help him catch up with the children in his reading group, who had read several preprimers since Patrick had left the group.

We began with *Rhymes and Tales*, Level 3 in the Holt Basic Reading Series. When Patrick visited me he said, "I have this book. I already know the stories." He then read the stories to me. When he had finished reading I asked him if he would read the stories to his teacher.

* When Claudia read this, she said she felt it was important to state that it was not just that Patrick's stories were not counted in the evaluative process. She said, "They were not counted at all by [name of first-grade teacher] when she was working on a day-to-day basis with Patrick in the classroom."

"I don't know."

"Would you like to?"

"Not really."

"Does she know that you can read this?"

"Yeah."

"Mmm?"

"Yeah. She knows that I can read that because, um, I have that in my reading group. I used to have it but, um, they are probably done with that book."

"I think they have done with that book, Patrick, but—"

"They were on this book." He picks up another preprimer that is on the table.

"Well," I say, "they are going on to the one that's in my living room."

"What one?"

"There's one more of these, but we can read this one in the next week or so."

"They're going on to the next one?" he asks.

"Mmm. Mmm. I think so, because I think you've been out of the group for a little while, haven't you."

"A long time," he whispers. "Can you get it?"

"Mmm, but let's look at this one first, though. Tell me about your reading group."

"I don't know why they, um, put me out." He whispers. "They just did."

"Was it hard?"

"Yeah." Patrick's voice trembled.

"How do you feel when you're asked to read?"

"It's just that, um, I don't do very much other things that other people get to do."

"Why don't you get to do them?"

"Because I'm in a different [inaudible]. I'm in a different [is silent for a moment] reading group than them."

"Does that make it difficult?"

"For me because I, um, already had that book."

In the following weeks we read together *Ask Mr. Bear* by Marjorie Flack, and Patrick read *Whose Mouse Are You?* by Robert Kraus, *Thump, Thump, Thump* by Ann Rockwell, and *The Carrot Seed* by Ruth Krauss. One Friday early in March, we gathered together all the books that we had read to reread them. Patrick sorted the books into piles.

"Only these books. These books we're going to read," he said.

"This one we have to read too." I tried to give Patrick one of the preprimers he had been reading.

"No. I read that one."

"Well, we can read it together."

"I don't want to read that one."

"Why not?"

"Because I don't like those books."

Patrick read the story books that we had gathered, but he did not read the preprimer. Claudia said that at home he also refused to reread them. Many of his books he read over and over again, but the preprimers he read once and then never returned to.

On March 31, 1987, a meeting was held at Patrick's school to review his progress. In his notes of the meeting, the director of special education states:

Rdg. is presently *ok* in a 1-1 but not yet ready for a group. Dictation is coming along nicely. 1st grade is now doing four sentences as is Patrick.

Mention is made of the preprimers that Patrick had read, but what is not mentioned is that his teacher requested that the books be returned to the school in case he was "memorizing the stories." It was also stated that he would need them the following year if he was retained in first grade.

The concluding paragraph of the notes written by the director of special education states:

While having improved in class in many ways, the single characteristic that distinguishes him from other students is his difficulty working independently —this too is somewhat improved.

On his third quarter progress report Patrick received an "Outstanding" for "Works well with others" and a "Satisfactory" for "Works independently."

His teacher wrote:

Patrick continues to find the first grade tasks difficult. He is beginning to read and he is beginning to show some greater readiness in the writing area.

The preprimers were returned to Patrick's teacher, and although he continued reading the books in school for the remainder of the school year, he did not rejoin his reading group.

Out of school, Patrick's whisper became quietly more confident, and the more he read the more audible he became.

On April 21, 1987, I was injured in a biking accident and was unable to work with Patrick for almost six weeks. During that time, the decision was made by the school that Patrick should be retained in first grade. Claudia and Pat refused to give their permission for the retention, and their relationship with Patrick's teacher became extremely fragile. Claudia said that in one conversation with his teacher Claudia was told that the only reason that Pat refused to allow the school to retain his son was Pat's ego. In the same conversation, Claudia said, the teacher stated that I had "muddied the waters." There was less and less contact between Patrick's parents and the school. Claudia said that in the end all the school wanted to discuss was retention, coding, and retesting.

Towards the end of May 1987, I began to work with Patrick again, reading books and writing stories. It was at this time that he wrote the following story:

Once I saw a big flower. It looked like a tree. It had flowers on it so I started to climb it. Oh! I was little so I got down. But a cat came. It saw me. I ran as fast as I could up the tree. Then a bird came and picked me up so the mean cat would not get me. He took me [to a] bigger tree and I was happy and I stayed there for a minute. Then he took me on a mountain. Then I lived there with the bird and we built a house and we made a living room and a kitchen. And I went swimming in the pond and the bird did not go swimming. He read. We lived happily ever after. The End.

On his fourth quarter progress report, Patrick received another "Outstanding" for "Works well with others" and a "Satisfactory" for "Works independently." His teacher stated:

Patrick continues to be developing his academic skills at his own pace. He is a super little boy and we must all continue [to] help him with his self image. We will wait to make a placement for the next year until we hear from you.

Summer 1987: Emmett's Pig

O n June 30, 1987, Claudia and Pat received a "speedy reply message" from the school district. The subject was Patrick's placement for 1987–88. It stated:

Have you obtained any more information regarding Patrick's placement for next year? Will you please notify the [name of school] office by 8/11/87 if you plan to retain Patrick or place him in second grade? [Name of the Director of Special Education] will be your contact person during the summer if you choose to have Patrick evaluated.

The message ended with the telephone number of the director of special education.

During the summer I worked with Patrick twice a week. Our goal was to help him with his reading and writing so that he would be more confident in school when he entered second grade. Mostly we focused on reading so that he would be placed back in a reading group when he returned to school.

In July 1987, Patrick read *Ask Mr. Bear* by Marjorie Flack. When he finished the book, he was smiling. He asked me to drive him home to tell his mother how well he had read the book. That summer we also read *Funnybones* by Janet and Allan Ahlberg, *Little Bear* by Else Holmelund Minarik, and *The Little Red Hen* retold by Margot Zemach. Patrick found a copy of *Old Mother West Wind*, by Thornton W. Burgess, in my office. He struggled to read the story and then asked if he could take the book home. My husband, David, recorded some of the stories, and Patrick read a few of the tales. Then Patrick's grandfather came to stay. They enjoyed reading *Could Be Worse!* by James Stevenson. Patrick often reread this book, and we frequently joked about everyday events by saying, "Could be worse!" Another favorite became *Alexander and the Terrible, Horrible, No Good, Very Bad Day* by Judith Viorst. After reading this book, we often talked about moving to Australia.

On one occasion we visited the town library, and Patrick chose ten books that he would like to read. One of them was *Emmett's Pig* by Mary Stolz. The next time Patrick visited my home he brought *Emmett's Pig* with him. He sat at the table and talked about the book.

"You don't know this, but—um—I picked a book that I wanted to read, and it was this one, and I read until here [turns page and points] to there."

"You've read all that yourself?"

"Yes."

"To yourself, or to your mom and dad?"

"To myself."

"That's terrific. So you've been doing some silent reading. Put the book on the table so I can see it too, and you can pull your chair up a bit. So this book is—what's it called? *Emmett's Pig*? Okay. Where are you going to start? Do you want to tell me the story so far?"

Patrick turned back to the beginning of the book. "I want to read it. Okay. I want to read this book until I can read it so well that [pause] that I can read it so well that I can read it any time that I want."

"I think that's terrific."

Patrick turned the pages. "I read it until there and I said, 'Should I keep going or not?' and I said, 'Okay, I'll go.' But I read it until there and then started to read here."

Patrick read. After a few pages he stopped. "Now this is a real tough page," he said.

"That's a lot of words, Patrick!"

"I want to read it."

"You can do it."

"I can read until here," he said, turning the pages. "I'm going to read this whole book!"

Later, when Patrick had finished reading the story, he talked about his cousin. He said that his cousin was sixteen and he had just passed his driving test. Patrick then incorporated this information into a story about Emmett:

Emmett lived in the country. Emmett was 16! His mom and dad lived in Florida. They liked it. Emmett said, "I will get a car." Emmett got a motorcycle with a roof and sidecar. He bought a house.

In preparation for Patrick's return to school, I constructed a biographic literacy profile (Taylor, in press), which presented a detailed description of his observable literacy behaviors. Two observations were included that were based upon the reading of *Emmett's Pig* and the writing that he did based upon that story:

Reading: Patrick reflects upon what he has read and he makes connections between present texts and texts read earlier in the year. For example, when Patrick was reading *Emmett's Pig* he read that Emmett "sat up in bed." He paused and then said, "that's like *Funnybones*." Patrick went on to make the connection for me. "Sat up in bed," he said, and he went on to explain that the Big Skeleton in *Funnybones* "sat up in bed."

Writing: Patrick edits for meaning. He rereads or asks for a rereading of the piece that he is writing and changes words to fit the story. For example, when Patrick wrote a story about Emmett he began a sentence with "It," referring to the motorcycle with a sidecar that he had written about in the previous sentence. He changed "It" to "The" and then, after a few moments' hesitation, he changed "The" to "He" and continued to write about Emmett, "He bought a house."

When Patrick came to read and write with me, one of his parents usually stayed. We didn't realize it at the time, but their presence made a difference. Patrick refused to read to them at home, so it was only during their visits that Claudia and Pat were able to hear him read. Then towards the end of summer, Patrick began to read at home. Claudia and Pat observed the progress he was making, and they became convinced that he would be able to continue his education in second grade. Patrick seemed to grow taller as he read books and wrote stories. He always seemed to be smiling when he arrived at my house. He would tell stories about his family, and then he would turn his baseball cap around, settle into a book, and read. Sometimes, after he had worked for about an hour, he would go outside and throw sticks for my dogs. I would follow with Claudia or Pat and we would talk about the next school year. Patrick had made so much progress that summer. He had become a self-confident young reader, and, I think, for a short time, just before second grade, he really believed that the more he read, the easier it would get. Claudia, Pat, and I would say this to each other as the books Patrick read piled up on the table. Like Patrick, his parents and I also believed that the more he read, the easier it would get. With all the pieces seemingly in place for him to continue with his education, we began to talk of phasing out Patrick's visits to my house. On several occasions I told Pat and Claudia that I didn't think he would need to visit me after September. We spoke of a transition period, and of my providing support through the first few weeks of school, until he was settled in second grade.

In late August 1987, the literacy profile that I had written was sent to the school. Following the description of Patrick's observable literacy behaviors, I had made several recommendations to "assist Patrick and his teacher as he begins his second-grade year." In first grade, Patrick had been removed from his classroom early in the morning, just as the other children were settling into their morning routine. It seemed important to recognize that Patrick had never been given the opportunity to establish such a routine, so my first recommendations focused on the organization of the classroom:

It would be extremely helpful during the first few weeks of the new semester if Patrick could receive support in gaining a good understanding of the social organization of his classroom. He will need to be observed carefully to ensure that he is familiar with the daily routine of his room and can function comfortably within that setting. I would advise that Patrick be given a written copy of the schedule so that he can use it at school and perhaps talk about it at home.

During the initial weeks of the semester Patrick should be present during all classroom activities. It is especially important that he be present at the beginning of each day when the schedule is discussed and work assigned.

Recommendations were also made with regard to reading and writing:

It is extremely important to build instruction on what Patrick already knows about oral language, reading, and writing. I would advise that instruction focus upon meaningful experiences and meaningful language rather than on isolated skill development.

Every effort should be made to ensure that Patrick feels successful in accomplishing the tasks that are assigned to him. It is important that the emphasis be placed upon what he gets right and not what he gets wrong.

Second Grade: Testing the Effects of the Testing

O n September 8, 1987, Patrick entered second grade. He was placed in a reading group and given the basal reader that the rest of the children had been reading at the end of first grade. It was nine months since he had last read in a group situation, and the children were reading the last story in the book. At the end of the first week of school the children in his reading group were given an "end-of-book comprehension" test. Patrick's teacher telephoned Claudia and said that Patrick had been unable to complete the test. Claudia talked with her and told her that Patrick had not read the preceding stories and that he was not used to the format of the test. Patrick's teacher was sympathetic and concerned. But she also talked about being a new teacher in the school and, because it was only her second year of teaching, she felt that she should refer Patrick to the child study team.

Claudia asked for the test. A few days later, when Patrick came to my house, I asked him to read the story that was at the top of the page. Patrick got off the chair on which he was sitting and stepped back from the table. "It's *not* a story," he said. After a few seconds he began to read, stumbling through the first few sentences; then, relaxing a little, he read more fluently. When I asked him to tell me what he had read, Patrick had no difficulty recalling what happened. Later, as we settled into reading other stories, Patrick talked about reading. He said: "If you reread, it makes you think more. It doesn't help you sound it out. But it helps you think the word out and you get more sense out and it can help you sound the word. I think it's good to reread over because you can practice more. You can practice a lot and it helps you.''

On September 25, 1987, the referral was written. The reason for the referral was given as follows:

Lack of phonetic attack skills:
—can not sound out the appropriate letter sounds and blend together to form a word.

Patrick therefore can not read [''phonetically'' inserted in text] which further leads [*sic*] that he cannot comprehend what he is reading. Patrick can comprehend what is read to him.

Patrick is placed in the lowest reading group [*sic*] however his group is now up to a new level. Patrick is not able to keep up in this new level.

Under ''Other remarks'' was written:

- Difficulty processing directions and information given step-by step and repeated.
- Handwriting skills—lack of pencil control, lack of spatial relationship between letters and words.

It was at this time that I telephoned the principal of the three small elementary schools that included the school Patrick attended. I talked with her about the reading and writing Patrick was doing out of school, and I requested that his second-grade teacher be given the opportunity to visit and observe him in what the school referred to as the ''tutorial setting.'' The principal denied this request, saying that it was important that the teacher form her own opinion of Patrick's reading and that the reading he was doing individually with me was not directly relevant. She stated that Patrick had to read in a group situation in school. I asked if I could provide an audio recording of Patrick reading; I was advised not to do so. The principal was polite and explained that the teacher was new and very conscientious. She said that she did not want to add to her responsibilities at the beginning of a new school year. She then talked about the school's ''legal obligation'' to make referrals and of the ''strict process'' that had to be followed. Then she assured me that Claudia and Pat would be informed ''all the way along.''

On October 9, 1987, Claudia and Pat received a handwritten progress report written by Patrick's teacher. She stated, ''We are all aware of Patrick's academic situation, so I will not comment on that. It is important, however, to note that Patrick appears to be very comfortable in the classroom. He gets along well with all of the students and is well liked. . . .''

On October 14, 1987, the referral meeting was held at the school.

The director of special education reviewed the "history to date" and asked Patrick's teacher to talk about Patrick. She stated:

Patrick has difficulty reading a complete sentence. When he reads he is unable to complete a sentence. Patrick has become the student who underlines and circles, but there appears to be little comprehension. He doesn't seem to be able to sound out words. He has difficulty getting through a sentence. As we get into second grade there are very few activities that don't involve reading. Reading is a real roadblock. He has difficulty sequencing. When he looks at a word I don't think he's seeing what I see. When he sounds out he doesn't seem to be pronouncing the sounds.

The subsequent discussion focused upon coding and testing. Because Patrick's first-grade year had been so difficult, Claudia asked if he could have extra help. She asked about Chapter One but was told he didn't qualify. The director of special education said, "I don't think it's possible to provide an individual program in a public school. It's not possible to receive extra help without coding, and coding cannot take place without testing."* He went on to state that he thought Patrick had a "language-based learning disability," and to establish whether this was the case he recommended the administration of the WISC-R, the Detroit Test of Learning Aptitudes II, and the Woodcock-Johnson Psycho-Educational Battery. In addition he recommended "an individual measure of achievement," which he stated "would provide a comparative score with other students" and a formal classroom observation. The meeting was coming to a close; no one had asked about Patrick's reading and writing out of school. Pat asked if I could talk about the work Patrick had been doing with me. I then played an extract from an audio recording of Patrick reading. When I switched off the recorder, Patrick's teacher said, "That's not the same child. I have never heard him read like that." It was the first time that we had been able to establish that Patrick could read. For a moment Claudia and Pat smiled at the director of special education. "Doesn't this make a difference?" Pat asked. "How can he be coded with a language-based learning disability when you've heard him read?" The director of special education said that they would continue with the testing. In his notes of the meeting the director wrote, "Mrs Taylor . . . offered a recording of Patrick's reading that is impressive. A real dilemma." In a letter to Claudia and Pat dated October 23, 1987, he wrote, "We also need to resolve the dilemma of Patrick being able to read well out of school but not in school."

* *Coding* is the local term used to describe the process of designating a child for special education services.

On November 15, 1987, I telephoned the director of special education and asked if it would be possible for Patrick to receive special help until a decision was reached as to whether or not he was "learning disabled." The director stated that no extra help could be given without coding, and then he explained, "It is exclusively the purview of the team to decide whether a child be coded educably handicapped, and that's done based on testing."

In a conversation a few days after the referral, Pat talked about reading with Patrick. "Patrick read to us," he said. "I can't believe that no one will listen." Pat talked about a technical paper he had just read that was written by one of his old college professors. "It's about trees," he said, "but it applies to Patrick. Instead of trying to find out what makes a tree sick, let's find out what makes a tree healthy." He gave an ironic laugh. "We're always looking for the worst." Then quickly he added, "So far this week he seems in good shape. Every night he reads *to me*. It's beautiful. It's exciting. It's not just one book. He reads one, then I read two. I let him stay up if he wants to read. I don't stop him. I let him go for it. I'm amazed." Pat talked of Patrick sometimes having trouble with little words. "He's stumbling because he's ahead of himself," he said. But then the excitement was gone and Pat sounded anxious. "If he's tested and they put him in a phonics program he'll be fit to be tied." Pat talked on about Patrick and the ways in which his needs should be met in the classroom. "That's their job," he said emphatically. "There should be some way of aligning professionals." Then he added, "We haven't done anything that any reasonable parent wouldn't do. The most frustrating thing is that the public system is supposed to give a child a good education. Somewhere, somehow, things have gone wrong. A lot of children are being shuffled and they shouldn't be shuffled."

I asked Pat about the referral. "Are you going to sign?" I asked.

"I don't think so," he said. Then he added, "I don't think we can."

We talked again about Patrick reading at home. Pat said that he was recording Patrick reading and that Patrick didn't mind. Pat said that on one occasion Patrick had asked his dad why he was making the recordings and Pat said, "I told him, 'Think when you are twenty and you listen to these tapes of when you were learning to read. That's classic stuff, Patrick! Classic stuff!' " Pat said that Patrick looked at him, smiled, and then went on reading.

Claudia also talked about Patrick's interest in books. "He's reading so much! The other night he read to himself for a whole hour."

But the difficulties that Patrick was experiencing in school began to take their toll. On one occasion when he visited me, his voice did not rise above a whisper, and he did not want to read. Claudia stayed and we looked at a story that Patrick had written when he first came to visit me. It was a pattern we established at that time. Patrick's vitality faded; we no longer said to each other, "The more we read the easier it gets." There was no point. At school, reading became increasingly difficult, and writing became a few sentences copied from the board or a fill-in-the-blank workbook page.

On November 2, 1987, the special education director wrote to the Commissioner of Education requesting an "Impartial Due Process Hearing." In the letter, the director stated that Claudia and Pat "have taken no action with regard to the local special education services team's 'Parental Permission for Assessment' form." The last paragraph stated:

The local special services team seeks permission to complete an evaluation designed to determine whether Patrick is educationally handicapped by virtue of being learning disabled and also designed to better understand Patrick's ability to read well out of school, but not while in school.

Claudia and Pat continued to talk with the consultant for the Bureau of Instruction for Elementary and Secondary Services. On November 6, 1987, the consultant said she had again telephoned the Superintendent of Schools. She stated that the superintendent "would not entertain the possibility of helping Patrick without testing and coding." Later she added, "He refused to discuss the matter at all, saying that doing so would undermine his relationship, or his loyalty, to his special education director."

On November 13, 1987, Pat and Claudia received a letter from the special education director outlining the mediation process that is sometimes used to eliminate the need for a full due process hearing. The director's letter stated, "Nothing is binding without mutual agreement."

In Patrick's school file are some notes dated November 16, 1987. At the top of the page are the names of two members of the special education section of the State Department of Education, the special education director and the coordinator of the elementary reading program. Beneath their names it states, "Re: Patrick ———." There is nothing else written on the paper. On November 23, 1987, Claudia and Pat met with the two members of the special education section of the State Department of Education whose names are written on this piece of paper in Patrick's file. I also attended the meeting. The officials, a man and a woman, were friendly, sympathetic, and kind. They expressed their disapproval of the rigidity of the position adopted by the school district and their concern that there were so few options available for Patrick. They asked, "What would you like to see happening?" and "What's the next step?" The discussion focused upon the possibilities of an independent evaluation, which would mean further testing. Pat was visibly upset by this suggestion. He said, "I don't buy it. I cannot agree to something that is fundamentally wrong just because the school system holds all the cards." Pat went on to say that it amazed him that even though these people were from the State Department of Education, they had no authority to act on Patrick's behalf. It was a long meeting. At the end of it, one of the officials talked about what we had accomplished and wrote down that at the meeting we had discussed options. We had, but nothing had changed, and the situation remained the same.

On November 30, 1987, Claudia and Pat received copies of information booklets on special education mediation from the special education director.

On December 1, 1987, a memo was sent to Claudia and Pat from the director of the Special Education Mediation Program. There would be two mediators. Claudia, Pat, and I were listed "FOR THE STUDENT." The special education director and the coordinator of the elementary reading program were listed "FOR THE SCHOOL DISTRICT." The date was set for December 9, 1987. Claudia and Pat were told that they should "plan to stay for the full work day."

Claudia and Pat spent most of their time in the following week trying to gather as much information as they could about the mediation process, about testing and coding. They made phone calls to the State Department of Education. The notes that they made as they talked reflect the concerns that they had about the school district's treatment of Patrick. Claudia wrote the questions that she wanted addressed on a piece of paper. Among the questions were "How are test results going to be in an environment that he is having trouble in? Will it give you the true picture?" She wrote, "It has been shown that Patrick is reading out of the classroom. Why test for a language-based learning dis.?" Later in the notes she stated, "We don't want him coded for a problem he may not really have."

On December 9, 1987, Claudia, Pat, and I traveled together to the State Department of Education. On the way we talked about our families. Nervously, we laughed and shared stories. Patrick had just had his eighth birthday and Louise, my daughter, had made him a chocolate birthday cake, complete with candles, that she had given him while he was visiting our home. Claudia said that when she was driving Patrick home, he said to her, "Louise didn't have to do that. She didn't have to make me a cake, because she's sixteen and I'm just a little kid.'' Claudia said that on the day after Patrick's birthday he had come downstairs and said, ''There's no more seven-year-olds in this house.''

I have no notes of the mediation process. We all signed a secrecy agreement, so I put my note pad and audio recorder away. After the meeting the director of the special education mediation program congratulated Claudia and Pat on reaching an agreement, but on our way out of the building Pat said he wasn't happy. We drove into town and parked the car and went in search of somewhere to eat. Claudia cried as we walked along the street. We tried to joke about silly things, things that had happened to us, to our families, and to our friends, but the more we tried to close out the events of the day, the more quickly we were drawn back into them. At one point, Claudia encapsulated our thoughts when she said, ''Nobody wins. All we can do is compromise.''

In the mediation agreement that is now part of Patrick's record it states that the school psychologist will ''administer the WISC-R test.'' It also states that it was agreed that the 1986 and 1987 group testing results of the California Achievement Tests be used ''as a criteria for current level of performance.'' An updated literacy profile I had prepared was to be included, and the district's learning disabilities specialist was to observe Patrick both in his classroom and in the tutorial setting at my house. The document ends by stating:

An individual evaluation plan will be written in the event that Evaluation Team determines that Patrick is Educationally Handicapped.
An individual achievement test, the nature of which will be determined by mutual agreement . . . will be scheduled in conjunction with the first I.E.P. update assuming that Patrick is determined to be educationally handicapped.

On December 14, 1987, I talked to Claudia on the telephone. I asked her how things were going. She said, ''The last few days have been awful. On Thursday I wanted to be by myself. I went Christmas shopping. But I couldn't shop. This is the worst Christmas for me. If we said we were taking him out of school, we'd have to go to court, because that would mean we'd win and they won't let us do that. The more you think about it, the more it bothers you. We're going to collect all the information that we can on the WISC and present it to [name of special education director].''

On December 29, 1987, Claudia and Pat met the school psychologist who was to administer the WISC-R to Patrick. I attended the meeting. Briefly, Pat presented a history of the situation and told the psychologist why they wanted to meet him. The psychologist listened and responded to their concern about the large number of tests that Patrick had taken. In my notes reflecting on the meeting I wrote that the psychologist said that

working with a child over a long period of time was the ideal form of assessment. But then he talked positively about I.Q. testing. It was a pattern that he set up and maintained throughout the conversation. The way things should be and the way things are. "Morality" versus "legality"—those were his words. He was cynical and jovial, laughing at his own cynicism. "The government doesn't want students to think too much," he said. "That's why so many bright kids have trouble in school." We moved between testing and the way public education is set up. Children are tested and coded so they can get the help they need. We wait until the problem becomes severe. We don't prevent problems, we remediate—ours is a therapeutic system. . . .

At one point during the morning the psychologist talked about Cadillacs and Chevys. He said that public schools did not provide Cadillacs, just Chevys, and that even with extra help it might not be enough.

During a telephone conversation in late December, Claudia talked about Patrick and about a story he had written during his last visit to my house. "He's been giving that story to everyone to read. We tell people that when Patrick writes he focuses on the story and not on the spelling, and Patrick agrees, and he seems quite comfortable with that."

The story of which Claudia spoke was called "The Peas." Patrick wrote two versions of the tale. The first was quite short:

One day, while I was eating my peas I heard a noise. It was [a] pea. It said, "don't eat me. I was shocked."

The second version expands on the story:

Yesterday while I was eating my peas I heard a noise. It was my peas. I looked down and my peas said in a low voice, it said, don't eat me! I ran off to my mom, I said my peas said to me, "Don't eat me?" My mom looked at my peas and said, "I don't see a pea speaking." Then she left. I heard another noise. It was an army of peas!

Patrick was tested by the school psychologist on January 7, 1988. On the way home Patrick said he had asked "the man" if he could play chess. Patrick said the man said no. Patrick then said, "I told him I can." Attached to the report that Claudia and Pat received on January 12, 1988, is a breakdown of the "Similarities subtest" noting the following as "psychoeducational considerations":

1. Understanding simple associations and relationships.
2. Concrete and abstract thinking (low & high order).

3. Semantic relationships.
4. Fluency of verbal expressions.
5. Expressive language skills.
6. Capacity to extract essential concepts.
7. Concept formation (rigidity-fluidity).
8. Use of imagination and fantasy.

Through an examination of Patrick's story "The Peas," we could have developed an analysis of the complexity of Patrick's use of these "psychoeducational considerations." However, this was never a possibility. Instead, the Similarities subtest was noted as indicating a weakness in "verbal concept formation," which, the psychologist stated, when combined with a weakness in "simple assembly skills," suggests "inflexible thinking, poor abstracting abilities, concrete thinking and visual-motor disorganization."

More disconcerting to Claudia and Pat were the statements made by the psychologist about the validity of the tests. He stated:

Patrick's scores within and across subtests showed significant scatter. In the former he got easy items wrong and more difficult items correct. Just when he seemed to fail a sequence of items necessitating termination of a subtest, for example, after 4 wrong in a sequence, he'd get the 4th [*sic*] one correct thereby beginning the sequence again. Also, his range of scores was 10 points since he had a low score of 3 and a high score of 13. Thus, the validity of this test is strongly questioned, especially those lower subtest scores.

Claudia and Pat asked, "If the test isn't valid, would the school insist on another test?" An even more urgent question was whether the recommendations made by the psychologist would lead to the school's returning to mediation for an agreement to conduct the further testing. The psychologist's report stated:

Further evaluation will need to be done in these areas:
1. Neurological screening to rule out ADD.
2. Projective testing to determine emotional interference in cognitive functioning, and if so, its potential sources.
3. A thorough LD evaluation.

"How can he write all this if he thinks the test isn't valid?" Claudia asked. Then she added, "We're in exactly the same position as we were before. The test hasn't made any difference." Claudia was visibly shaken. She said she had gone to the district office to pick up the report and then she had sat in a nearby pancake restaurant to read it.

She said, "When I read what the psychologist had said about Patrick I
began to cry."

I observed Patrick in his classroom early in January 1988. The
observational record began at 8:30 A.M. and concluded at 11:45 A.M.
The following is an excerpt from my notes that I submitted with a
report to the child study team:

8:55   The teacher says, "Phonics." They talk about the page that they
        have reached. Then the teacher talks about the words. She instructs
        them to put their finger under the first word. She says they're *k-n*
        words. "Think of a *k-n* word."
        Someone says, "Knife."
        The teacher talks about instructions, listening and following
        directions. "Everyone listen one more time to this voice."
        The teacher goes through the schedule for the day.
        Patrick gets up to go to the bathroom.
        The teacher tells him to sit and listen.
        He sits back in his seat.
        The teacher finishes talking.
        She says, "Let's keep the green light on." (At the front pinned to
        some construction paper on the board is a green paper circle, like a
        traffic light. Below are two more circles, one orange and one
        yellow.)
        "You can talk quietly, move about, but be considerate of others."

9:04   Patrick goes to the bathroom.
        Some of the other boys say they need to go when Patrick gets
        back.

9:09   Patrick comes back and sits down.
        The other boys go out one at a time.
        The teacher walks over and talks with Patrick.
        Patrick nods. The teacher leaves, and he starts working in his
        phonics book.
        Someone walks over and looks at the poem that the teacher has
        written out and given to Patrick. Another child joins them. They
        leave.

9:10   Patrick is looking at the page in his phonics book. He gets up and
        takes the book to the teacher and asks her about one of the
        sentences "Cathy _____ some red-and-white socks").
        The teacher demonstrates the meaning and talks about making
        sweaters. Patrick says, "Oh," and begins to leave.
        The teacher puts out her arm to stop him.
        She smiles and says, "What is it?" She demonstrates again.
        Patrick says, "Knit."

9:12   A child goes by Patrick's desk.
        Patrick asks him one of the words at the top of the page.
        The boy looks, pauses, and then says, "Knitted."

9:14   Patrick is looking around. Then he returns to his book.

9:15   The teacher speaks to the boy sitting next to Patrick.
        The boy says Patrick asked him about a word.
        The teacher tells him to get on with his work.
        Patrick returns to his book.

9:17   Patrick is looking at his book. He rolls his pencil over the page.
        Then he holds up his book and asks the boy next to him what
        something says.
        The boy whispers.
        Patrick nods and goes back to his workbook page.
        The teacher is working with a reading group. They are talking
        busily as they work. Patrick is looking at his book.

9:20   The boy who has been helping Patrick comes over and gives me his
        book. He says he can't do one. The word he needs is *written*. The
        sentence reads, "The note is neatly _____."
        I ask him how you make a note. He says, "You write." He looks
        at the words at the top of his phonics page. He says, "Oh." I
        say, "Which one?" He points to *written*. On his way back he
        passes by Patrick's desk and shares the information. Patrick works
        in his book.

9:25   Patrick is up. He has a cut-out shape and goes to the back of the
        room to get some paper. Then he walks over to the reading corner
        and takes a different shape.
        The teacher is up. The reading group children are back in their
        seats. The teacher is walking around the room, talking with
        children and looking at work.

9:28   Patrick is back in his seat. He draws around the heart shape and
        begins copying the spelling words from the board around the edge
        of the heart. The teacher speaks to him. He gets his reading book
        and workbook.

9:30   Another reading group, including Patrick, gathers around the reading
        table. Patrick is sitting with them. He is next to the teacher. They
        talk about the story they read recently—*The Middle Is NO Place
        To Be*.
        Patrick listens and joins in the conversation.
        One of the children has trouble finding the page. Patrick leans
        across the table and helps her.

9:35   The teacher reads. Patrick is looking a little in front. He looks as if
        he is listening, but he is not looking at the print.
        The teacher says, "There are two people who don't get to go
        anywhere." A child says, "Pablo." Patrick adds, "Carmen."

They talk about going places. Patrick talks about going out to
play without his sister.

9:38   Another child reads.
The teacher follows with her finger down the lines in Patrick's
book. Patrick is not looking at the print.
The teacher asks for "another volunteer."
A child reads.
Patrick appears to be listening, but he is not following the lines
of print.
Then Patrick reads. He hesitates and stumbles a few times, but
he reads the page without difficulty.
The teacher fills in the few words that give him a problem and
in this way she helps him maintain the flow of the story.
The teacher tells Patrick that he read well.

9:43   Another child reads, and then another.
They have all read.
A child asks if they can finish the story. She volunteers to read.
The teacher checks to make sure that everyone has had a turn. She
asks Patrick to read.
Patrick reads using his finger as he reads across the line. He
reads word by word but with increasing expression in his voice. The
teacher helps him with one or two words, but this time he is
reading on his own, comfortably, and in a clear voice.
Patrick sounds confident as he reads, and there does not appear
to be a big disparity between him and the other children in his
reading group. Several children read more fluently, but one or two
appear to have more difficulty than Patrick.

9:50   The children are talking about the zoo and making a zoo train. The
teacher has a construction paper boxcar with zoo bars. Patrick tells
the teacher about the animals he has seen, and then he talks about
their cages and the doors on their cages.

9:51   The teacher explains how they're going to make a zoo train. The
children look at the outlines of the zoo animals. They can choose
one to color and cut out—to put in their zoo train.
Patrick chooses an elephant and then swaps it for a crocodile.
The teacher finishes talking about the zoo train and asks the
children, "Who has done their phonics?" She looks at each of the
children in the reading group. Patrick does not have his hand up.
When the teacher looks at him he says, "I can't get it. It's too
confusing." He tells the teacher that he has been working on his
"Spell-a-ma-doodle."

9:55   The children return to their places.
Patrick goes to the bathroom. He comes back quickly, and the
teacher joins him by his desk. She looks at his phonics workbook
page.

"Good job so far. Did you get some help? Everyone is in trouble with this one."

Coincidentally, the story that the children in Patrick's reading group were reading during the observation was the basalized version of Judy Blume's *The One In the Middle is the Green Kangaroo* (see Goodman 1988). Patrick had read the original, and more complex, Blume book both with me and with his parents at home. Claudia said that he really enjoyed the story. She said that when he first brought the book home, he read well past his bedtime, because he wanted to read the whole book. "We talked about Freddy," Claudia said. "He talked about Freddy moving in with Mike and about his mom and dad saying, 'It's the boys' room.' " She then added that they had had a long conversation about the meaning of the statement "But they couldn't fool Freddy."

On January 19, 1988, the learning disabilities specialist observed Patrick in his classroom. However, no report was received until March 1, 1988. The mediation agreement had also stated that the learning disabilities specialist was to observe Patrick reading and writing in what the school called the tutorial setting. But no arrangements had been made. Claudia eventually called the special education director and made subsequent calls to the learning disabilities specialist before arrangements were finally made for her to visit my home on February 11, 1988. The report of the observation was not received until March 3, 1988. Claudia was present during the visit of the learning disabilities specialist's observation. She went over the stories that Patrick read and the story that he wrote during the observation. We wondered what the specialist would report. "I tried to put myself in her place," Claudia said. "Just think how far he has come since last September. If I observed him I'd be impressed." But we had to wait until the beginning of March, and eventually Claudia would have to telephone the school to get a copy of the report so that we could read what the LD specialist wrote.

On March 4, 1988, I talked with Pat on the telephone. He began by saying, "The pressure is incredibly intense. We're tired. It's a catch-22. We just want the best for him."

Early in March 1988, another event occurred that added to the complexity of the situation. Claudia and Pat had asked on many occasions if Patrick could have extra help with reading through Chapter One, but they were told repeatedly that he didn't qualify.* In February

---

* On reading this account Claudia recalled that there were many reasons given: "They told us that there was no room, that the program was full, and that he was next on the list. But the main reason was he didn't qualify."

Claudia had learned from a friend that there were children receiving
help with reading through Chapter One who came from more affluent
families, and that there was even one child receiving this assistance who
was in the top reading group in Patrick's class. Claudia had spoken to
Patrick's teacher about the situation, and it was shortly after that he
finally began receiving help through the school's Chapter One program.
The effect was devastating. Patrick almost stopped reading entirely.
His voice dropped to a whisper, and he became upset at the least little
difficulty. "I'm really bothered," Claudia said. "I feel like packing my
bags. I have to find out what he's missing. She [Patrick's teacher]
made it sound as if [Patrick's[going [to the program] at 11:15. But I
was in there and he was out at 9:00. Usually, I don't go in that early."
Claudia paused, then talked about Patrick's reading at my house earlier
that day. "When he was reading I could have cried." Knowing that
earlier in the year Patrick had been reading easy chapter books and that
stories such as *The One in the Middle is the Green Kangaroo* had been
easy for him to read made it really difficult for Claudia to watch as he
struggled to read a few pages from a book with just a few words on
each page.

There was no doubt that our meetings had changed. Most of the
time we spent talking and sharing stories; sometimes reading, but
mostly just talking. Sometimes we were silly, sometimes sad. Patrick
did not talk much about what was happening to him in school, and we
did not question him. We just hoped that the time we spent together
talking and reading stories would help him. "When I've seen what I've
seen in the last few weeks," Claudia said, "I don't know what to do."
She had learned that, during the time he was out of the classroom
receiving extra "help" through the Chapter One program, Patrick was
just working on more phonics dittos and workbook pages. "Patrick
is just getting more of the same thing," she said. "If that's what's
happening, if she knows he hates it that much, how can she give him
more of it? That's torture." Claudia said, "I get upset. I get cold and
start shivering. I want to just grab Patrick and Elizabeth and Pat and run
away. And disappear. It's a terrible feeling to just want to run away.
It's kind of a lonely feeling. I just keep trying to get my faith back in
human beings. But why can't they see what is happening to Patrick and
children like him?" Later in the conversation Claudia said, "It's beyond
any kind of comprehension. I feel betrayed. They're going to do it
[code] anyway."

Claudia and Pat tried to cope with their sense of powerlessness by
educating themselves about special education, testing, and learning
disabilities. They studied *The Learning Mystique* (Coles 1987) and read
The Magic Feather (Granger and Granger 1986). Pat used his computer

to access research on assessment stored in ERIC, and my files and bookshelves became resources that they used in learning more about early literacy. But time went by slowly as they waited for the school reports of the observations to be written and for the date to be set for the child study meeting. Sensitive to the potential difficulties that many children face through inaccurate kindergarten screening programs, they became interested in a bill being considered by a house subcommittee on education that advocated the "diagnostic screening" of all children on first entry to school.

On March 15, 1988, I went to the state capital to testify at one of the subcommittee hearings, and Claudia decided that she would accompany me. She was the last to speak. Reading from the statement that she and Pat had stayed up until 2:00 A.M. the night before preparing, she spoke of Patrick's preschool screening, and then she read the list of tests that he had taken since that time. She said:

The supposed reason for these tests was to find out why our son didn't read as well as the other children in his first-grade classroom and to find if there was a learning disability. It should be noted that these tests did not identify a specific problem. In addition they offered no clues as to possible instructional methods to improve his reading. In fact, along with the negative approach from his first-grade teacher, there was severe emotional trauma to the point where his self-esteem was almost nonexistent. At this point, school became extremely unpleasant and not the learning environment that it should have been.

The family stress that these events have created cannot be taken lightly. For us, it has been mentally and emotionally debilitating, and for our son it has caused emotional scars that will be with him for the rest of his life. . . .

It is time for parents, schools, and society to allow our children the freedom to enjoy learning, as they do instinctively, without labeling them on the basis of standardized tests according to statistical norms. . . .

School itself is very stressful for young children, and to be put through this kind of scrutiny is a crime that should not be allowed. Life is stressful enough for our children. We don't need to add to this by testing.

When she had finished speaking, several members of the house subcommittee talked to Claudia and expressed their concern. Later, Claudia said she felt that testifying had been worthwhile, because just for once someone had listened. But the moment passed, and she was still waiting, filling the last few days before the child study meeting rereading the reports written by the therapists and pathologists and trying to place these documents within the framework of the books and research papers that she had been studying. Pat also spent his time researching and reading, talking with members of the State Department of Education, and mostly just spending time with Patrick. His small business became a secondary concern, and he was unable to keep up with the work he should have been doing to meet the commitments he had made to clients who needed work. This meant that the family's financial situation became extremely fragile, for while the representatives of the school were paid for their time spent in preparation for, and for their attendance at, meetings, this was not the situation for the family. Neither Claudia nor Pat were compensated for the time they spent as they worked to represent the best interests of their son. Instead, they suffered a financial loss, and their small business was placed in jeopardy.

The learning disabilities specialist's school report finally arrived. It was a three-page document based upon two hours of classroom observation. Claudia was distressed to see that the report focused exclusively on Patrick. His behavior was not related to that of the other children in the room, and she felt it gave a distorted impression of Patrick's behavior. Claudia telephoned and asked for a copy of the report that the specialist had written about the observation of Patrick at my home, but she was told that it was being rewritten. Eventually Claudia went to the school and got the report. It was written on two pages, but could easily have been condensed onto one. Of the story that Patrick wrote (a story about the Red Sox—see Figure 3), the LD specialist reported:

Patrick then told Mrs Taylor that he began writing a new story last night. He wanted to continue writing it. Patrick sat and thought for a few minutes. He asked how to spell "once." Patrick immediately remembered that the word was in *Teeny Tiny*. He found it in the book and copied it onto his paper.

As Patrick completed a thought, Mrs. Taylor would read it out loud. Patrick whispered the words he was writing as he wrote. He appeared to be sounding them out. At one point he wrote "ben" for "being." When the sentence was read aloud to him that way, he corrected the spelling.

Patrick noted that when he writes he will put the first letter of a word down and then follow it with the first letter of the next word in his mind. He said, "I do that a lot."

As Patrick wrote, he never verbalized his thoughts prior to putting them on paper. But, as was noted earlier, he sub-vocalizes as he writes.

Occasionally a word would be pointed out to him as missing a letter. Patrick would identify the missing letter and add it.

However, the whole story was not assessed for spelling errors. When he finished the story, it was re-read and he was praised for the quality of his work. Throughout the whole lesson positive praise was given. Mrs. Taylor pointed out to Patrick that she had spelled a word (at his request) for him, and when he used the word later in the story he didn't need to see it again.

Figure 3   Patrick's Red Sox Story

once I went to a
baseball game The
redsox lost. I went
houme and went to
SleP. I dremd uBaot
Bening in The baseball
game. The neKs t day
I wen t to ce nuthr
game I Prtedi nd I
Was in The game
I Prtedi nd Tha
baseball ga me! na
The Wun The ^

(Continued)

Figure 3   (Continued)

Prt2

The baseball game

was over I ~~Prtedi~~

Prtedin so hard That

The redsox wun in

~~rel~~ life I was

gad Tha wun!

It was a tiren

day I ned to

gow home and go

to bed The nex

day I stad nom

Figure 3 (Continued)

and flayd baseball
with DaD I hit
a home run
and Then I hitthe
ball ucros the stret
DaD hit a DoP
fli I cot it
you aer dowt
I sea to him
I wes uP alsgen
I WUN

I also wrote a description of the literacy behaviors I had observed during Patrick's production of the story in Figure 3, which I subsequently incorporated into the literacy profile update that the mediation agreement stated should be included in the information to be considered by the child study team. My analysis is presented below:

This personal narrative opens with a topic sentence and proceeds with the development of the opening idea in terms of Patrick's experiences at a baseball game. It is a multilayered story in which Patrick moves back and forth between reality and fantasy (he imagines watching the Red Sox and then playing for the Red Sox). Patrick continues balancing imaginary events and real-life situations throughout the story, until he ends it by incorporating into his narrative his own experiences of playing baseball with his father (when Patrick wrote that he hit the ball across the street he commented, "That was true. I did that"). Patrick's production of the story clearly indicates the sophistication of his cognitive abilities, the flexibility of his thinking, and his considerable skill at incorporating abstract ideas into his production of written texts.

In this story Patrick presents a logical, orderly progression of ideas. Using the entire page, Patrick demonstrates that he understands how stories are constructed and how they are put down on paper. He has spaces between his words, and he is beginning to demonstrate his understanding of sentence structure and punctuation. Patrick has also begun to revise and edit his stories (e.g., in the baseball story he wrote "They won" at the bottom of the first page of the text and then he decided to change what he had written to "They won the baseball game!" To do this he inserted "baseball game" above "won").

His spelling is rapidly moving from invented to standard in a very normal progression. His use of initial and final consonants is almost totally standard. There are a significant number of vowels in the words that he writes, and it is clear that Patrick is sensitive to the often idiosyncratic patterns of double vowels in the English written language (e.g., ub*aot*—ab*ou*t). His representations are not yet standard, but the patterns in his writing make visible his understanding. Patrick also incorporates other high-level substitutions into the words that he uses in his stories (e.g., ne*kst*—ne*x*t), and he is confident in the use of invented spelling to symbolize words that he has not yet learned to spell (e.g., *prtedind—pretended*).

Patrick demonstrates that he has a large number of sight words that he can use when writing stories and, in writing this story, he demonstrates a few of the strategies that he uses to find troublesome words that he wants to write. For example, Patrick found *once* in a book that was on the table. He also asked, "How do you spell baseball?" I responded, "Do you want me to write the word?" Patrick replied, "Yes. Write the word." It should be noted that once Patrick had been given the word *baseball*, and he had used it in his story, he then went on to write it from memory. During the writing of this text, Patrick also gave some indication of his metacognitive (I prefer metalinguistic) awareness of his own emergent literacy behaviors when he commented, "Oh! I always do this. I write the first letter and then I go on to the letter that is at the beginning of the next word." In this way Patrick has learned to monitor his own progress in writing, and he has been able to make the shift from stories written using predominantly invented spelling to stories that are predominantly written in traditional orthography.

My own role in the production of this particular story (and his stories in general) was minimal. Patrick writes quietly and rarely needs encouragement. There are times when he will write for an hour or more, and he sometimes continues writing when he gets home. The assistance that I provide is often no more than pointing to a word and asking Patrick if he hears any sounds that would indicate the presence of another letter in the word (e.g., pointing at the *sa* that Patrick had used at the beginning of *stayed*—Patrick said "T," and added the letter). This is a simple example of the zone of proximal development. Patrick usually already has the information he needs, and a simple question helps him gain access to the information.

The staffing meeting was set for March 17, 1988. The notification stated that the meeting was arranged "to determine, based on available information, whether an educationally handicapping condition exists." Claudia and Pat were still concerned about the psychologist's report and tried on several occasions to speak to him during his visits to the school. Eventually Claudia managed to reach him by telephone. She asked him if he was going to talk to them about the report before the meeting. Claudia said, "He said, '[name of special education director] can do that.' I said, 'You make recommendations and then someone else interprets them?'" In his report the psychologist had mentioned *The Hurried Child*, and he had suggested that Claudia and Pat attend a "parenting education/child development" program. Claudia said, "I don't think it's right that he can say we need to take a parenting course and that Patrick should have a full neurological and then not have to look us in the eye." Claudia finally arranged to meet the psychologist before the staffing meeting, but little else was done or said to help her as she prepared for the response to the WISC-R test that she expected from the special education director.

During the time that I worked with Patrick throughout his second-grade year, I spoke regularly with colleagues whose research focuses upon the literacy development of young children, learning disabilities, and special education. Gerald Coles of the Robertwood Johnson Medical School in New Jersey and William Wansart in the Special Education Department at the University of New Hampshire both provided continuous support through their willingness to listen and discuss the many educational implications for Patrick of the events that were taking place in his life and in the lives of his parents. Donald Graves of the

University of New Hampshire also provided support, and it was to him that I turned on the evening of March 15, 1988. I telephoned Don and asked him how he thought Claudia and Pat should approach the staffing meeting. Except for a brief time in first grade (see Taylor 1988), we had been unable to get the special education director to take into account that Patrick *could* read and write, despite the test results to the contrary. The special education director had made statements to this effect in letters that he had written both to Claudia and Pat and to the Commissioner of Education; however, the official position of the school remained unchanged: Patrick had a language-based learning disability. How could we get the special education director to listen? Don suggested that I develop a series of questions that each participant at the meeting be asked to address. "What is the purpose of the meeting?" Don asked. He stressed that it was important that all of the participants agree on what information was to be used in the decision-making process. "Until there's agreement on evidence, there can be no discussion," he said. "What's Patrick's perception of the batteries of tests that he's taken?" Don continued, "What is Patrick's perception of what has happened? Ask 'What is the purpose of the meeting?' " Don paused. "If it's to code this child, then the decision is made." Based upon my conversation with Don I made a list of questions:

For all participants:

1. What is the purpose of this meeting?
2. What is the purpose of your participation in the meeting?

For the participants from the school district:

3. What is your perception of the parents' concerns with regard to the evaluation of their son, Patrick?
4. What are Patrick's perceptions of the batteries of tests that he has taken and of his school experience in general?
5. In what ways have you (as individuals) worked with Patrick?
6. If you have worked with Patrick, what are his academic strengths? What are his weaknesses?
7. If you have no experience of working with Patrick, what is the basis for your participation in the decision-making process that is taking place today?

For Patrick's parents:

8. What is your perception of the school district's concerns with regard to the evaluation of Patrick?
9. What are Patrick's perceptions of the batteries of tests that he has taken and of his school experience in general?
10. What are Patrick's academic strengths? How would you describe the ways in which he learns?

11. Based upon all the above information, do you feel comfortable with the purpose of the meeting and the participation of each member of the child study team?
12. How would you like the meeting to proceed?

For the school district:

13. Is the structure of the meeting established through these opening questions acceptable and are you ready to proceed?

On March 16, 1988, I gave the questions to Pat and Claudia and suggested that they think about them, advising that they either use them as a basis for the questions that they would ask at the meeting or, if they felt it was appropriate, make copies and share the questions with all of the participants at the meeting.

On March 17, 1988, the staffing meeting took place in Patrick's classroom. The special education director, the resource room teacher, the learning disabilities specialist, Patrick's second-grade teacher, Claudia, Pat, and I attended the meeting. When we arrived Pat asked if the special education director would mind if I recorded the meeting. He stated that he had no objection, so I took my audio recorder out of my bag and placed it in the middle of the table. Before the recorder was turned on the special education director began the meeting. He stated that the purpose of the meeting was to determine whether Patrick was "educationally handicapped." (The following is a transcript of the remainder of his opening statement.) He stated, "That's the purpose of the evaluation meeting, and in accomplishing that I've put together the evaluation summary, and it enumerates the information that we have." He paused. "Now we are looking at Patrick from the perspective of being learning disabled, therefore educationally handicapped—that seemed to be the most likely constellation of issues that would explain his learning patterns, given the state guidelines, and what we have to do in that case, to demonstrate that a learning disability exists is to demonstrate that there is in fact a significant difference between his learning and his ability."

Pat said, "Mm-hmm."

The director continued, "and that is why we wanted to have a measure of intellectual functioning to get some idea of where ability was and also a measure of achievement to find out roughly how much he knew."

Pat coughed.

The director continued, "Now the measure of achievement we agreed when we went to mediation would be the most recent achievement test so as not to put Patrick through any more individual tests."

Pat said, "Mm-hmm."

The director continued, speaking to Claudia, "So this right here is that, Claudia. See, that's a copy of that."

Claudia said, "Mm-hmm."

The director repeated, "So that's a copy of that."

Claudia spoke, but it is inaudible on the tape.

The director continued, "Now this is the summary. Now you have a copy of [name of the psychologist]'s test results?"

Pat said, "Mm-hmm."

The director said, "Okay."

Pat moved in his seat. All of the school's evidence was now on the table. The California Achievement Test results, the psychologist's WISC-R, and the "Evaluation Summary" that noted both these tests and also mentioned the observations that had been made by the LD specialist and me. The reports written to describe these observations were referred to as follows: "Several observations have been completed which show Patrick to be making a sincere effort on behalf of his own learning."

The director of special education began to rearrange these papers on the table. Pat sat up straight and began to speak: "I would like to say one thing, [name of director], before—"

The director interrupted. "Sure."

Pat continued in a controlled voice, "Before we go on, err, the question is—we're basing this on simple test scores. In order for us to get a full handle on this, we have to go through these questions that we want to have addressed so that we know exactly where we all stand. Is [there] a common ground here—you know what we're talking about and we know what you're talking about. That's what I'd like to do."

The special education director stated that he had answered the first question and I asked "if that was the common consensus of everybody." The director spoke of state guidelines and he stated, "That sequence has to be adhered to."

Pat said, "As far as we're talking about decision-making process, we're involved in the decision-making process—"

The director interrupted. "Sure."

Pat continued, "And in order for us to get our points across without yelling and screaming at everybody, I think I would like to go through and ask each person here to describe and answer some of these questions. We'll answer the questions too and let you know how we feel."

The director sat, holding the paper with the questions.

"Perhaps you'd like to read them through first, [name of director]," I suggested.

The director looked down at the paper. "Yes," he said, and then for a moment he read. "Okay," he said. "I really came unprepared to deal with this. I would really have appreciated it ahead of time."

Pat responded, "Well, I understand that, and I respect that."

The director said, "Mmm."

Pat continued, "However. We are talking about making a decision about Patrick's situation, and these [points to the questions] are very important that they have to be addressed by everyone in this room because we can't just base this on an individual achievement test or a WISC-R, especially when we know other information, and what we've been through and Patrick's been through." He paused. "I think you know it's a reasonable thing to ask. I don't think it's asking anything excessive from anybody." Pat paused for a second and then he looked at the director and, saying his name, he asked, "You know, have you worked with Patrick?"

The director answered, "No, I haven't."

Pat said the name of the special education teacher, "You've worked with him?"

"I've seen him within the classroom," she said.

Pat persisted. "How many times have you worked with him?"

"I haven't," she replied, "because it has never gone to the point where I, as a special ed person, could work with him."

Naming the LD specialist, Pat asked if the specialist "has ever worked with him."

"I've observed him," the specialist replied.

Claudia again spoke, but it is inaudible on the recording.

"Okay," Pat continued. "So what we're talking about is we're basing this meeting and this evaluation on this test here and this WISC-R. Is that correct?"

The director replied, "And I think, Pat, on two years of experience, of three years of experience now almost in the public schools."

"Three years of Patrick's experience?" Pat asked.

The director said, "That's right."

"Yes?" Pat persisted.

"And the staff," the director replied.

Pat looked at the second-grade teacher. "Is Patrick not functioning to his level? Is that what we're talking about?"

"Patrick's having [*inaudible*] having trouble. He could, I know he can do better." She coughed.

The discussion continued, with Pat asking about the lack of "cross-referencing" between what Patrick was doing in and out of school. The issue of Chapter One was raised. Pat stated, "He's only just started getting Chapter One."

The director brought the discussion back to the question of coding. He stated, "We want to make help available to Patrick. We'd like to do that. We're prepared to do it. But in doing that we've got to follow special education procedure."

"Okay," Pat responded. "Now let me get this correct now. He's going to be considered, coded, learning disabled for what category?"

The director spoke calmly. "I think that if we're collectively agreed with the information we've collected about Patrick we can in fact code him learning disabled."

"For what?" Pat and Claudia asked almost in unison.

"For being educationally handicapped," the director answered.

"For what?" Pat persisted.

"In what category?" Claudia asked.

"Language," the director answered. "It's a learning disability category in the state of [name of state]."

The discussion continued, with Pat talking about Patrick reading with me out of school and the work not being taken into consideration. The question of Chapter One was again raised, and then Pat spoke angrily of the psychologist's report. He said, "In addition, [name of director], I think it's preposterous for you to come in here and discuss [name of psychologist]'s report. He is the one who should be here right now."

Claudia began, "We want—"

Pat interrupted. "I can't believe this."

Claudia continued. "We want to know why this man is not accountable for his recommendations in that report. I think that those recommendations are not founded."

The director again spoke calmly. "You misunderstand, Claudia. He can make any recommendations he wants."

"Based on what?" Claudia's voice was raised.

The director spoke quietly. "Based on his experience."

Pat interrupted. "What, forty-five minutes with Patrick?"

The director spoke quickly. "No, no, no—er, let me finish. He can make any recommendations he'd like in his report, as a psychologist in the state of [name of state] that are reasonable with the report." The director paused, then continued. "Those recommendations do not have to be followed."

"I realize that," Claudia said.

"It's this team of people—" the director began.

Claudia interrupted. "I realize that."

The director continued, "—team of people who make that decision."

Claudia began again. ''I realize they don't have to be followed, but I also—'' She stopped speaking.

I asked, ''Is that report being used in the decision-making process, [name of director]?''

He replied, ''Only some of the information, I mean.''

''Even though—'' I began.

''At this point, Denny,'' the director took over, ''What I'm looking at is to find a difference between ability and achievement to the extent that we justify coding.''

''Even though the psychologist himself says that the test is invalid?'' I asked.

''I think we can draw some conclusions from the test even though that—'' The director stopped and the tone of his voice changed. ''He didn't say it was invalid.''

The discussion continued as Pat looked through the psychologist's report to find the relevant statement. Finding it, he reads, ''Thus the validity of this test is strongly questioned especially those lower sub-test scores.''

''That's right,'' the director stated. ''And the conclusion that I would draw from the scores, Pat, is that Patrick is at least this intelligent. He's [*inaudible*]—''

''Well,'' Pat interrupted, ''I mean, exactly. So. But you can't base anything on that. If you say that the—''

The director took over. ''All I have to do, all I have to demonstrate is that there is a difference between Patrick's ability, or his lowest level of ability, and achievement. That is all I have to do.''

''What does the test show you?'' Pat persisted. ''I mean really show you.''

The director began, ''The test [*inaudible*]—''

Pat interrupted, calling the director by name, and then began, ''I tell you. I really—''

The director continued, picking up where he had left off. ''It tells me that Patrick is at least this intelligent—''

''Right,'' Pat said. ''So. What is that going to tell us? We've been through—wait. I just want to read. I would like to read this. Just so we have it. Where is that.'' Pat searched through the papers that he and Claudia had brought with them, looking for the statement that Claudia had read at the subcommittee hearing on diagnostic testing. Both of them looked through their papers but were unable to find it.

It was at this time that I asked the director about the lack of accommodation in Patrick's program to his learning needs. Claudia and Pat continued to look for the statement that Pat wanted to read, but the director did not wait. He stated, "We can proceed in one of two ways, and I'm willing to do either. We can either proceed with the coding on the information that I have, or I will take a list of what you think would be helpful for Patrick and implement it the best I can while a due process goes through the procedure to determine his condition."

Pat suggested that Patrick's second-grade teacher work with me to coordinate the work that he was doing in and out of school. The director resisted and stated that was not up to him. Pat protested as the director continued, "The kinds of things I have seen work with Patrick is the extra exposure, the introduction to materials prior to being introduced in class, the reinforcement of those materials. The—um— the ability to verbalize those materials and experience them in greater depth than he does in the regular classroom. I've seen those kind of things happening with Denny. I think that those are the kinds of things that really help. Um. So. We can provide that kind of thing in school. The reinforcement."

"Well, I think—" Pat began.

"Reinforcement of what, [name of director]?" I asked, interrupting.

"His basic curriculum here," the director replied.

The discussion continued until the director spoke with finality, "I'm willing to provide additional reinforcement every day in his basic curriculum. Math and reading. Err. He can continue with Chapter One. But I am not willing to change the curriculum dramatically on the face of the evidence that we have."

"Even though you know that this child is writing much more complex texts than he is reading in his basal reader?" I asked.

"I'm not sure that I know that," the director replied.

The discussion continued. The questions had been ignored. The reports were never discussed. The specialists never spoke, except to answer Pat's questions about whether or not they had worked with Patrick. All that counted was the director's interpretation of the test results.

"Well, as I said," the director spoke, driving his decision home, "we can proceed one of two ways. We can proceed with the special education procedure and get Pat help that way, or we'll be willing to reinforce his curriculum that he has now and then let the due process hearing officer settle it."

Angry and tired, we continued. What had begun as a discussion became an argument, filled with our short-tempered frustration. But the director remained calm.

"Where would you like to take today?" he asked Claudia and Pat. "What would you like to do with it?"

Pat replied, "Well, it's obviously not going to be coding. So. I guess it's due process. That's fine with us."

"Okay," the director replied.

"Because, er—" Pat began.

"I'll file for the due process and send you," the director stated, cutting Pat off. He had stood up and was packing his briefcase. For a few last angry moments the discussion continued as Claudia, Pat, and I tried again to get the director to consider Patrick's work.

In the final interchange the director said, "We have to code them if they are educationally handicapped according to state guidelines." Then he concluded the meeting with, "I'll send you all the information you need to know."

"Fine," Pat replied.

The director said thank you to the school's child study team and walked out of the room.

The LD specialist and the special education teacher followed the director of special education out of the room, but Patrick's second-grade teacher stayed, and we sat in silence, disabled by the meeting and unable to speak. After a few minutes Claudia talked about testifying at the State Department of Education, and Pat asked her to read the testimony that she had given. Claudia began to read. When she reached the list of tests she started to cry, but she continued reading, clearly and deliberately, the name of each test that Patrick had taken. Then, when she had finished, she dropped the testimony on the table. Patrick's teacher spoke of her second-grade classroom and said that she wanted to do more to help Patrick. She said she had expected some kind of resolution after mediation, but that it was now March. At one point, Claudia asked her if she had read the report of the observation that I had made in her classroom, and she said that she had never seen it. She said that she had not seen any of the reports about Patrick and explained that the director of special education had told her at the beginning of the year that he would try not to get her involved. Claudia went through the papers that she had brought to the meeting, and she gave a copy of my observational notes and the accompanying report to Patrick's teacher. We talked for a while about Patrick learning in school, and it was at this point that his teacher stated that he was "learning on his own." In my notes of that meeting, I wrote that she said that she knew Patrick "doesn't learn from the way basals and phonics books expect him to learn, so what he's getting he's getting in another way." We talked of trying to make "small adjustments" to workbook exercises to provide Patrick with the opportunity to complete his school assignments in ways that made sense to him, and we spoke of giving him some options: "You can do it this way, or, if you'd prefer, you could try this.'' But I think we all knew that these suggestions were too little, and too late.

It was almost six o'clock in the evening when we left the school. As we prepared to leave Claudia said, ''I knew it would come to this,''

''Code or court,'' I said, remembering what she had said earlier in the week.

She nodded bitterly, and then she managed to smile. Pat stood beside her and put his arm around her for a brief moment, and together they left the room.

Due Process:
Code or Court

n the weeks that followed the referral meeting, I met with Claudia and Pat almost daily, working with them as they tried to prepare for due process. On March 20, 1988, we worked through the evening and into the early morning, trying to unravel the legal ramifications of the school district's "code or court" position. Claudia was concerned about the inadequacy of the summary statement given to them by the director of special services at the March staffing. That the observations of Patrick were mentioned in a cursory sentence upset her, but she was also concerned about the rest of the document, for it just did not seem to present enough information on which to base the coding of a child. Pat studied the special education regulations, reading aloud the statements about learning disabilities and testing. Claudia related the statements that Pat read to the statements made in the mediation agreement and to the information that they had on "impartial due process" hearings. Together they sifted through their files, rereading letters and reports. Claudia found a statement on "Parental Rights in Special Education," and she questioned whether or not the director of special education should have read them their rights at the referral meeting. On through the evening, reading phrases such as "no single procedure" and "data should be current," looking up laws and interpreting subsections, we tried to place Patrick's situation within the context of the laws and regulations governing schooling and special education. Pat would say, "Listen to this," and then "Read this," as he sifted through the papers, cross-referencing and asking questions.

As we worked, Claudia and Pat also talked about the impact of the school's decisions upon their family life. "The law has got to be changed," Pat said shaking his head. "We've had two terrible days, but we're coming out of it." Claudia said that on the day after the referral meeting she had difficulty walking. "I couldn't put one foot in front of the other," she said. Pat talked about his business, and said that he was unable to concentrate on it. It was spring, and he said that he needed to start hiring people and making financial plans for the upcoming year, but that he just couldn't focus. Claudia said that Pat was also physically affected by the difficulties that they were facing. She said that they had gone out for breakfast on Sunday and that Pat was so low he had come home and just lain on the couch until Patrick and Elizabeth finally coaxed him into playing with them.

On March 31, 1988, Pat and Claudia received a copy of the letter that the director of special education had sent to the Commissioner of Education (dated March 25, 1988). In it he stated:

The local special services team feels that Patrick is educationally handi-capped, but has been unable to productively involve the parents in making this decision. Thus, we request a determination by a hearing officer.

Claudia and Pat said the letter made it sound as if they were doing nothing to support Patrick. Pat said, "All the Commissioner has is [name of director]'s letter. He doesn't know what's going on." It was at this time that Claudia and Pat decided to write to the Commissioner of Education to ask for an investigation, and over the next few days they worked on this letter.

On April 3, 1988, Claudia telephoned and said that a pre–due process hearing had been scheduled for April 25. We talked about the work that needed to be done before the hearing, and then Claudia talked about asking the school to remove Patrick from Chapter One. Claudia said she had asked Patrick if he liked Chapter One and he had said no, and then had asked Claudia if he had to go. Claudia said that she told him that he didn't have to if he didn't like it. She said that he didn't say anything else, but just got up and left the room. Claudia continued by saying that Patrick had come back after a few minutes with some paper and a pencil. She said he had sat down at the table and started writing a story. "It's the first story he's written since he began Chapter One," she said.

On April 18, 1988, Patrick visited me, and for the next two weeks we worked together each day. Claudia and Pat decided that an extra week added to the spring break would give him an opportunity to relax and, they hoped, a chance to regain some of the confidence that he had lost during the year. Looking through the books on the table, Patrick chose *The Day Jimmy's Boa Ate the Wash*. In my notes I wrote:

Patrick had not seen the book before. After looking through the pictures I asked him to read. He hesitated and substituted words (e.g., *corn*—which was in the picture—for *class*). After a few minutes I said I'd read it first. Patrick said, "Good." After I had read the book, Patrick read it to me. Hearing it made a difference. Undoubtedly it gave him some understanding of the story and a framework for reading, but I think there is more to it. New books appear to be like tests—unknown words to be decoded, strange sentences to be read, new information to be learned. Patrick visibly relaxed during the reading. He seemed to shift gears, reading some parts "automatically." A similar phenomenon happened in his writing. As he thought about *said* he wrote *se*, hesitated, added an *i*, and then a *d*. In the very next line he was moving quickly and he wrote *said* without appearing to think about it. I talked with him about the word and congratulated him on writing *said*. Throughout the remainder of the story he wrote *said*. Later, we talked again about his progress from *seid* to *said*.

On April 19, 1988, in a conversation about Patrick being out of school for an extra week, Pat said, "The house seems really different. We haven't been this calm in a month. He has accepted that he's staying out for the week. On Tuesday he said, 'I'm going to miss gym.' I said, 'We'll play baseball.' Patrick said, 'That's fine.' " Each morning Patrick worked with me at my house and then, while he was at home with Pat, Claudia and I spent the rest of each day preparing for the due process hearing. Like Claudia and Pat, I too found myself unable to think about anything other than the upcoming due process hearing. I was concerned that we were all being swept along by the events that were taking place, and I felt unable to keep a rational perspective. Reading Maxine Greene helped. In *Landscapes of Learning*, she writes of "posing our own critical questions to reality," and this is what I tried to do, on my own, with Pat and Claudia and with colleagues. Together we tried to gain some understanding of what was happening. I talked with Gerry Coles, William Wansart, Gay Su Pinell, Jerome Harste, JoBeth Allen, and Don Graves. I showed them stories that Patrick had written and shared the results of the tests that he had taken. Each of these researcher-educators offered their support and advice, and in different ways they each stated that they were willing to help—by writing to the Commissioner of Education or by analyzing test results and examples of Patrick's writing or by testifying on Patrick's behalf.

Overwhelmed by the complexity of the laws and regulations, Pat and Claudia decided to retain a lawyer to represent them. However, it took many phone calls to find a lawyer who would be willing to take the case. Most of the lawyers were tied up with other cases, and some said they did not specialize in educational law. Financially, Claudia and Pat were unable to pay for the extensive legal services, and so I tried to find a way of getting them the support that they needed without the crippling legal fees (one lawyer had stated that they would be between $10,000 and $15,000). I spoke with representatives from the American Civil Liberties Union, The Children's Rights Center at Harvard Law School, and The Children's Defense Fund in Washington. Those with whom I spoke were concerned and helped by suggesting other advocacy groups that might be in a position to provide assistance, but after a week of telephone calls I was unsuccessful in finding a way for Claudia and Pat to receive the help they needed. Eventually, a lawyer was found, and Claudia and Pat met with her for the first time three days before the pre–due process hearing, which took place on April 25, 1989. (The following account is based upon my notes and what can be heard on a faint audio recording of the meeting.)

At the pre–due process hearing the hearing officer talked about dates, documents, and defining issues. He stated that the party bringing the appeal begins, and witnesses testify under oath. The other party then cross-examines. The discussion focused on rules and regulations.

The director of special education then stated that over a two-year period the school has been concerned about Patrick and his learning. He stated, "We attempted to meet on March 17." The hearing officer listened and eventually questioned the director: "You are saying that he does not have a learning disability?"

The director said, "No. I think he has."

The lawyer retained by Claudia and Pat stated that the school had not been meeting Patrick's needs. She asked, "If Patrick's needs are not being met adequately and coding is not appropriate, then what is appropriate?"

The director stated that he thought we should focus on the special education issue and not the broader issues.

Claudia and Pat's lawyer said she wanted "to keep it open."

The director stated that he wanted the hearing in one and a half weeks. Claudia and Pat's lawyer said that there were expert witnesses to prepare and that she couldn't be ready within that time frame. The director stated that he wanted to invoke the forty-five-day rule. The discussion went back and forth—about dates, not about Patrick. The director stated, "I want to point out that if the school district were in that bind they would be expected to meet the deadline." The hearing officer suggested June 7 or 8. The director addressed the lawyer. "Do I understand that you would appeal any decision made within forty-five days?"

"Yes."

The director stated that it was not the school system's fault that Claudia and Pat could not make the forty-five days. The hearing officer said, "This is not productive." He stated that it didn't make any sense to go forward with the case if Claudia and Pat's lawyer was not given time to prepare. The hearing officer asked the director if he would agree to June 7 or 8.

The director stated, "I'll agree depending upon the agreement of *my* lawyer."

The discussion then focused upon expert witnesses and the possibility of using reports to limit expenses. The director stated that he could not agree to any expert statements without the opportunity to cross-examine. He added that he was concerned about the scope of the hearing.

The hearing officer then raised the issue of documents presented by the school. He stated that often they are not accompanied by the experts themselves.

The director stated that all documents would be supported by witnesses.

When I talked with Claudia the day after the pre–due process hearing she said that she and Pat had ended the day reading with Patrick and Elizabeth. At three o'clock in the morning Pat had waked her in Elizabeth's room, where she had fallen asleep. Pat had also fallen asleep in Patrick's room, and the lights were on throughout the house. What I remember in rereading my notes of this conversation is Claudia and Pat's deep concern that Patrick was getting lost in the legal skirmishing that was taking place. After a day of arguing about dates and witnesses, all Claudia and Pat wanted to do was spend time with their children. Looking back, I find it impossible to adequately convey the suffering that the family experienced. It was as real and as painful as any act of mental abuse that it is possible to imagine.

In the days that followed the meeting, I worked on a report to be submitted at the due process hearing. In the meantime, Claudia spoke with a member of the local school board, and Pat talked on several occasions with consultants from the State Department of Education. Letters began to arrive from the researchers and educators who had agreed to help. Several of these letters were sent directly to the Commissioner of Education. Gay Su Pinell, the director of the Reading Recovery Program at Ohio State University, wrote:

The program Dr. Taylor has designed for Patrick is consistent with the kinds of holistic interventions we have found to be so successful with young children. It appears that he is making significant progress in reading and writing, as evidenced by his writing samples and the texts he can read with high accuracy. His writing samples, in particular, provide evidence that Patrick is highly aware of letter/sound relationships and that he can use visual information to solve words. Dr. Taylor is working to help him learn to use this knowledge while reading extended texts. I have encouraged her to continue. My professional opinion is that these parents have selected a remedial option that is sound and can be supported by a large data base. I question whether many other remedial programs can report as much success.

JoBeth Allen, of the Department of Language Education at the University of Georgia, wrote:

When I listen to the tape of Patrick reading, self-correcting, comprehending, I learn that he has many of the strategies effective readers must have. I cannot think of a standardized test that would give me the same information as listening to Patrick read, in a variety of books over a period of time, in the kind of supportive environment where he has experienced success. If we are trying to evaluate whether children are learning to read, we must listen to them read.

Let me commend you and others working on Patrick's behalf for taking the time and care to assure his educational and social welfare. I spent two hours on the phone this morning with the leader in our state department of education, listening to her frustrations with policies and actual laws that she feels are detrimental to young children, but that she must work to make the best of. You are not in an easy position. I will be eager to hear how you resolve this situation for Patrick's sake, and for the precedent you will be setting for [name of state] and perhaps beyond.

Unfortunately, to the best of our knowledge, no action was taken by the Commissioner of Education. In addition to these letters (and another written by Donald Graves), he also received the letter that Claudia and Pat wrote in which they requested "a formal investigation regarding violations of agreements reached at mediation on December 9, 1987, and the overall handling of the situation concerning our son by [name of director of special education and director of the school district]." In reply, Claudia and Pat received a letter from the Curriculum Supervisor/Complaint Investigator. Ironically, this was the same person who had been in charge of mediation. The letter stated, "We will contact you concerning this complaint soon," but no further word was received regarding the complaint. Thus, as far as we know, neither the Commissioner of Education nor the school board member with whom Claudia spoke took any further action to investigate the situation. Claudia and Pat were legally left on their own, without any help from the system.

On May 20, 1988, William Wansart, Professor of Learning

Disabilities at the University of New Hampshire, evaluated Patrick by listening to him read and by observing him as he wrote a story. No tests were administered; instead, Bill videorecorded the session and used this recording and Patrick's story as a basis for his assessment. In a telephone conversation that took place on May 23, 1988, Bill said that he had found no evidence of a neurological disorder. He said that Patrick had more difficulties reading than many second graders but that his reading was not outside the normal range. "What's disturbing," he said, was that "he feels that now he's reading kids don't make fun of him. It's not a problem in his head, it's a problem in the school." Bill went on to state, "Realistically, there isn't anything wrong. Regardless of what the school says he's just a kid who is not reading as well as most second graders. There's nothing wrong with him, and I've worked with kids who have things wrong with them." Bill then talked about the Stanford Early Achievement Test and the Murphy-Durrell. "Why could he do these tests?" he asked. "Even within their own myth there's inconsistency." In another conversation several days later Bill talked about the findings of his evaluation. He stated:

Patrick was able to identify words that are spelled incorrectly. He wrote a typical first draft. He was very attentive and stayed on task. His oral language and his written language are good. He structures written language in sentences; has clear thought patterns; he had a beginning, middle and an end; and he had an interesting problem in his story. His writing is at least age appropriate for a language process classroom.

Bill then laughed and said, "His attention to task was good under the most distracting of circumstances," and he went on to talk about the way in which Bill had looked for another videocassette when the session had continued longer than anticipated. During Bill's search Patrick had watched him for a moment and then had continued working on his story.

In addition to Bill's evaluation, Jerome Harste, Professor of Language Education at Indiana University, and Gerald Coles, Professor of Clinical Psychiatry at the Robertwood Johnson Medical School in New Jersey, wrote reports analyzing Patrick's stories and the results of some of the tests he had taken. I used these reports in a document I prepared for the due process hearing in which I wrote as an advocate for Patrick and his family. The following presents excerpts from my report.

. . . No evidence has been found of any language-based learning disability. To the contrary, observations of Patrick as he reads and writes stories confirm that he is a highly articulate young boy who has a good control of spoken and written language. . . . There is no question that Patrick needs help in the continued development of his reading and writing and that his

reading is somewhat delayed in school. However, given the adverse circumstances of his schooling, it is to his credit that he has continued to develop his written language skills through his own efforts to read and write stories both at home and in the tutorial setting. Dr. William Wansart of the University of New Hampshire has evaluated Patrick, and in his *Assessment Summary* (attached) he writes of Patrick's reading:

☐ Given the lack of a consistent developmental reading program of instruction Patrick has made remarkable progress. While his reading ability would be judged to be below that of his current age or grade peers there is nothing developmentally atypical about it.

Dr. Wansart states of Patrick's writing:

☐ His story is very good. . . . This story would be typical of many second grade children in schools using the writing process. . . . His writing appears to be at least age appropriate.

Focusing upon Patrick's ability to attend and the possibility of "underlying problems" Dr. Wansart concludes:

☐ Patrick was able to attend for a sustained period of time and was not distracted by the unfamiliar environment or the activities in the setting. *No evidence of a neurological impairment* was seen in Patrick. Given the interruptions in his reading instruction and the stress and anxiety of repeated testing and of the due process procedures, of which he is surely aware, he has made remarkable progress.

Based upon my own long-term observations of Patrick and upon the perspectives presented by Dr. Wansart, Dr. Gerald Coles, Dr. Jerome Harste, and others, I can find no support for the concerns expressed in the documentation in Patrick's files. However, while these concerns tell us little about Patrick, they tell us much about the school. Patrick's files are filled with contradictory statements, which create an invalid and misleading record of learning disabilities. . . . Questions were raised about visual-motor problems, sensory integration problems, and temporal space orientation problems, and recommendations were made for therapy that focused upon tactile, visual, proprioceptive, and kinesthetic processing. Dr. Jerome Harste states:

☐ The problem with tests is that if we take enough of them finally a weakness is found. In most cases the data is redundant and the student who initially flunks a test or subtest is put in double jeopardy when given a second test.

There is no question that Patrick's academic life has been jeopardized by the test-retest syndrome that afflicts the school administration. A review of the tests that Patrick has taken in just two and a half years of schooling provides confirmation of this "code-the child" behavior. . . .

In light of the extraordinary number of tests that Patrick has taken, we are left asking whether Patrick's test behaviors are a learned response to the repeated questioning of his abilities in testing situations. As the school psychologist observed following his testing of Patrick in January 1988:

☐   He gave his answers impulsively instead of reflecting on them. His answers were practically out before the questions ended giving the interchange a likeness to College Bowl or ———— State Challenge.

Contrast this statement with what was written about Patrick in kindergarten in the report following the first administration of the Gesell Developmental Evaluation in March 1986:

☐   Needs time to deliberate and respond, to explore, experiment and finish. . . . Patrick works with a definite sense of purpose. He does his best and appears unconcerned with his errors.

Writing specifically about Patrick, Dr. Gerald Coles states:

☐   We have here a situation in which school personnel have been unremittingly looking for his neurological deficits, have been calling on outside agencies to help them when they could not find any themselves, have been focusing on what he cannot do, and have been almost perversely testing, retesting, and retesting again, determined to find the neurological "glitch" that will explain everything and exonerate everyone.

In first grade, to remediate the mythical glitch, Patrick was removed from his classroom early in the morning (when the other children were engaged in reading and writing activities) to work with an occupational therapist to increase both his gross motor skills and his sensory processing to "enhance classroom performance," and to work with the speech and language pathologist on color, size, and shape. Thus he missed valuable academic time and had difficulty completing his classroom assignments. This problem was "solved" at the end of the first semester when he was also removed from his reading group and was told that he did not have to copy from the chalkboard. In essence, in attempting to remediate a problem based upon what Dr. Gerald Coles describes as "spurious research," the school *created* problems for Patrick. Instead of receiving the *extra* reading and writing time such as that recommended in *Becoming a Nation of Readers*, *The Reading Report Card*, and *Who Reads Best*, Patrick received *less*. After reviewing both the tests that Patrick had taken and some examples of his schoolwork, Dr. Gerald Coles wrote:

☐   As I read the materials, I became increasingly distressed. Within this unwarranted school-created situation, can anyone expect Patrick's learning, motivation, self-esteem, and emotional well-being not to deteriorate—thereby effectuating the self-fulfilling prophecy that the school has been creating?

There is no doubt that Patrick is well aware that his abilities have been questioned by the school. At home, in the tutorial meetings, and in the evaluation conducted at the University of New Hampshire, Patrick has spoken painfully of his experiences in first grade. There is an entry in Patrick's folder that adds further insight into the deficit-driven pursuit of this child. At about the time that Patrick was removed from his reading group and was told that he did not have to either copy the dictation from the chalkboard or alphabetize his spelling words, Patrick started complaining of stomachaches and did not want to go to school. He refused to travel on the school bus, and he told his mother that one of the children was bothering him. Patrick's mother recalls that she talked to his teacher about the situation. Recently, in reviewing the documentation in Patrick's folders, his mother found the following entry:

☐   Would not sit in his seat—refused to get on the bus. Kids were not picking on him until he made himself different.

One wonders what this statement is supposed to mean. How does a young child "make himself different"? That such a statement could be made about this child or, for that matter, about any child is cause for serious concern, especially when the person who appears to have written the comment has stated that he has never worked with the child and only knows him from the documentation in his school folders. One wonders whether it is the child who is making himself different, or if it is the school system that is making him different.

The pursuit of Patrick (and, by extension, of his family) has been relentless, and it is no longer possible for me to believe that the school administration is acting in the best interests of this child. What has taken place is a travesty that cannot be condoned either morally or ethically. In writing about the coding of children for special education, Lieberman (1984) states that the vast majority of learning disabilities are *created*, not born. In the documentation in Patrick's folders it is possible to witness such creation in the slipshod accounts of the school life of this young child. It should be noted that:

1. Test data has apparently been ignored when it does not fit with a disabilities explanation.

2. Classroom observations are invalid, since no information is provided about the activities of other children in the room.

3. Contradictory statements have apparently not been analyzed, and no explanations have been provided of why such disparate information has been recorded about this child.

4. All information gathered in out-of-school settings about Patrick's language and literacy development has been completely disregarded.

In Patrick's second-grade year, modifications have *not* been made in the instructional practices used with him, even though his teacher has told Patrick's parents that he does not learn in the way that the basal and phonics books are set up for children to learn. In *Report Card on Basal Readers*, prepared by the Reading Commission of the National Council of Teachers of English, the opening statement reads:

☐   The central premise of the basal reader is that a sequential, all-inclusive set of instructional materials can teach all children to read *regardless of teacher competence*, and *regardless of learner differ-*

ences. It is all-inclusive in the sense that basals claim to include *everything* that any learner needs to learn to read [emphasis in original text]. (p. 1)

Much of this report on basal readers focuses upon the artificial control of the language in basals, and reference is made to the difficulties that this can cause for some children. The Commission states:

☐ [T]he evidence from science—recent theory and research—is that reading, like all language, only develops easily and well in the context of its use. The learner needs the freedom to experiment, to take risks, to raise questions in the process of trying to make sense of comprehensible written language. There is little choice, little self-control, little sense of ownership of their own learning and their own reading. (p. 125)

This is a critical issue. Through his reading and writing both at home and in the tutorial meetings (and more recently at the University of New Hampshire), Patrick has consistently demonstrated that his "disabilities" are context specific. Dr. Jerome Harste speaks to this issue when he writes:

☐ The other really interesting thing about the data sent to me is that it clearly demonstrates that P looks very normal in functional language settings; very "disabled" in settings where language is handled nonfunctionally.

Dr. Harste's comment adds support to the conclusion that it is the school's interpretation of how to teach Patrick to read and write that is disabling him. Dr. William Wansart of the University of New Hampshire, who recently evaluated Patrick, adds further support to the view presented by Dr. Harste. Based upon his evaluation, he states that Patrick was "very attentive even under distracting conditions." Patrick wrote a story during the evaluation that Dr. Wansart has described as a "typical first draft" that is "at least age appropriate," and that it would even be considered an appropriate first-draft production for a second-grade child working in a writing process classroom. Dr. Wansart stated that he found "*absolutely no evidence of neurological problems.*" . . .

In summary, what has happened is that a young child who had *apparent* difficulty with tasks such as cutting with scissors was suspected of having "perceptual problems." This led to close scrutiny of his abilities, and questions were then raised about whether or not he was "ready" for first grade. In first grade he participated on a trial basis and received extra "help" rolling clay, and identifying "big" versus "small," "round" versus "square." But while he was rolling clay and participating in similar activities, he was missing the opportunities to read and write in his classroom. It should therefore come as no surprise that he then had some difficulties in learning to read and write in the school environment. In December, to alleviate his "difficulties," he was removed from his reading group and was told that he did not have to participate in the classroom writing activities. He was therefore forced into a nonparticipatory role while still being expected to function in the classroom. When he entered second grade, he had not participated in a reading group for approximately nine months. At the end of the first week he was referred, ostensibly because he had difficulty with a comprehension exercise in a basal reader that the other children in his group had read while they were still in first grade. Since that time he has received no extra help except what has been called by the director of special education "reinforcement of the curriculum." To my knowledge the school has never asked (or even considered) the following crucial questions:

1. How does Patrick construct written language?
2. What are the similarities between the ways in which he uses print at home and at school?
3. What are the differences between the ways in which he is using print at home and at school?
4. How can we describe his miscues? What are the similarities and differences in his responses to miscues made at home and at school?
5. How can we describe his writing (invented spelling—traditional orthography) when he is writing at home and at school?
6. What writing strategies does he use at home and at school?

By ignoring these fundamental questions, the school ignores the child, it ignores the way he learns, and it ignores the importance of his learning to the development of his self-esteem. If the school is concerned about the long-term effects of their constant scrutiny and deficit testing upon the life of this child, it needs to reassess the consequences of its actions and to consider the ways in which it can help Patrick feel that it respects his ability to learn.

In concluding this report, I want to add my support to the statement made by Dr. Coles at the end of his letter about Patrick. Dr. Coles concludes:

☐ I find this sad case very dismaying. Rather than working on behalf of the boy and using valuable resources available to them, the school personnel seem to be going about the affair as though they were in a gunfight and afraid to blink. I cannot help but feel that Patrick may already have been seriously damaged emotionally.

I agree with Dr. Coles, and further support is added in Dr. Wansart's *Summary Statement* when he speaks of Patrick's deleterious first grade experiences plus the "anxiety of repeated testing and of the due process procedures, of which he is surely aware." I would urge the school system to reevaluate the position that it has taken and to begin immediately to try to redress the damage that in my opinion it has caused in the emotional and intellectual development of Patrick. In assisting Patrick in his literacy development "according to his needs and abilities," the school district will be doing nothing more than what is required of them by law.

When the report was finished, a copy was given to the lawyer representing Claudia and Pat. She advised that it should not be used until the due process hearing. Claudia and I continued working on the chronology that we were constructing of the documentation in Patrick's file, and made arrangements for expert witnesses. Donald Graves had agreed to testify; so had Bill Wansart. In addition, Gay Su Pinell had agreed to fly in from Columbus, Ohio, and arrangements had to be made for someone to meet her at the airport. Each day was spent in preparation, studying documents, listening to audio recordings, anticipating the testimony of the witnesses for the school district, and preparing examples of Patrick's work.

Then, on May 26, 1988, the lawyer representing Claudia and Pat telephoned to say that, on behalf of the school district, their lawyer had dropped the appeal. She said, ''They're in a bad position,'' and then she added that the school district was going to send Claudia and Pat a letter requesting further testing and that if the parents denied permission, the school district would again initiate a due process hearing. We discussed the difficulties we would have in rescheduling expert witnesses. Due to teaching commitments and vacations, it was unlikely that we would be able to get everybody together again that summer. The lawyer said that she did not think that the decision had been taken out of malice. She said the school district did not know about the arrangements that had been made for witnesses. She said that there was a difficulty with the documentation. She explained that not only was there a problem with the mediation agreement, but that at the March 17, 1988, referral meeting, the director of special education had not put into writing that the school believed that Patrick had a learning disability.

''We have been telling them all along that they don't have the right documents,'' Claudia said, her anger covering her grief. ''How can they turn it around and use it in this way?'' she shouted. ''Don't they know what they're doing to us? I won't let them test him.'' Gaining control, she talked about the director of special education. ''He doesn't care,'' she said. ''Otherwise he wouldn't be doing this.'' There was nothing else to be said. Numbed, we sat and drank tea. My daughter, Louise, came into the room and gave Claudia a hug. ''I could hear you upstairs,'' she said. Then she added, ''I'll teach Patrick,'' and Claudia managed to smile.

For a short while after that, Claudia and Pat tried to turn the suit around, but the process became overwhelmingly complicated and the legal fees were becoming as worrisome as the suit. At the beginning of June Claudia and Pat told their lawyer not to take the case any further. Emotionally exhausted and financially spent, they were unable to pursue the legal action any further.

Copies of letters were forwarded to Claudia and Pat by their lawyer and by the State Department of Education, but they never received a letter from the school district asking for their permission to retest Patrick. Perhaps the reason that that letter did not come can be explained by the letters that did arrive.

On May 3, 1988, the lawyer for the school district wrote two letters to the State Department of Education. In the first he stated:

> . . . [A] review of the documents involved in this case leads me to believe there is an issue which has not been brought to the attention of the hearing officer that may need to be resolved. That issue concerns a mediation agreement entered into by the parents of P. [last name] and the [name] School District on December 9, 1987.
>
> . . . In my opinion, the mediation agreement which arguably constitutes a binding agreement between the parties does not authorize the school district to obtain information which is adequate under the [name of state] standards and federal law to make a valid determination of whether or not the child is educationally handicapped. . . .

In a second letter, addressed to the director of the Special Education Mediation Program (who is also the person in charge of "complaints"), the lawyer frames his "comments" as "constructive criticism":

> The purpose of this letter is to express to you my concern regarding the terms of this agreement and the position in which it has placed the school district. Under the terms of the mediation program, this mediated agreement binds the parties to a course of action. Consequently, a question exists as to whether the school district is obligated pursuant to this agreement to code the child using only that information that can be obtained under the agreement and whether, if the school system believes the information obtained under the agreement is insufficient, it now has the right to request additional information. . . .
>
> . . . Furthermore I find it distressing that the mediated agreement specifies that individual achievement tests will not be administered to the student until the first annual review of his IEP which presumes that he has been determined to be educationally handicapped.
>
> I am sure that you can recognize the problems created by this mediated agreement. It binds the school district to a course of action which will provide it with insufficient information under the applicable [name of state] standards to determine if the child is educationally handicapped. . . . I believe it is not unreasonable to suggest that the school district is caught in a "catch 22" situation.
>
> . . . In short, this mediated agreement, if it constitutes a binding agreement as to the type of evaluation that will be performed upon this student, prevents the school district from fulfilling its legal obligations and prevents the type of informed decision making which the law intended to

assure. Since the parents are not expected to have expertise in this area, I am sure they entered into this agreement in good faith and have the right to expect it to be enforced. The school district may have felt some obligation to enter into what appeared to be a reasonable resolution of an ongoing dispute in order to enable it to hopefully provide services which it believed the child needed desperately. In my opinion, however, individuals from the Department of Education who acted as mediator in this matter should not have permitted the parties to resolve their dispute through an agreement which would not have led to information sufficient to enable a valid decision on whether the child was educationally handicapped or not to be made. . . .

On June 29, 1988, the director of the Special Education Mediation Program responded to the letter written by the lawyer representing the school district. She replied:

. . . It is not the responsibility of the mediators to proofread mediation agreements for illegal or noncompliant elements. As a matter of fact, [name of director of special services for the school district] has spoken to me about the [name of Patrick's parents] agreement and told me that he knew during the mediation session and at the time he signed the agreement which he had helped develop that a part of it was not in compliance, but that it had seemed to him to be the only way to move the case forward.

I would put it to you to advise your clients not to knowingly enter into agreements which they believe to be illegal or not in compliance with State and Federal regulations rather than to write to me and wish that the mediators would monitor a school district's actions.

Claudia and Pat waited, but no letter arrived requesting permission to administer more tests. There was no resolution except that Patrick's second-grade teacher told them that she could not recommend Patrick for third grade; he would have to repeat second grade.* Claudia and Pat were convinced that if they refused their permission for the school to retain Patrick the school would refer him and insist on coding, and then would reinitiate a due process hearing. "Code or court" were still the only options available. There were no private schools within commuting distance, and even if there were, Pat and Claudia would have been financially unable to pay for tuition. Exercising the only option left to them, they made the decision to home-school Patrick. They both felt that what Patrick needed more than anything else was time to get over the repeated questioning of his abilities. They were concerned that his experiences in school had threatened his emotional well-being as well as his intellectual development, but they also believed that he was school

---

* On reading the manuscript for this book, Claudia stated that she felt it was important to add that until this time the second-grade teacher had maintained that it would not be in Patrick's best interests to retain him in second grade.

disabled and not learning disabled in other educational contexts. Home schooling would give them an opportunity to help Patrick overcome the difficulties created for him by the school.

At the end of the summer they wrote a letter to the superintendent of the school district requesting permission to home school. In a subsequent meeting early in September 1988, Claudia and Pat met with the superintendent and told him what had happened to their son in school. Claudia said that he listened and appeared sympathetic when they spoke to him about the inappropriate behavior of both members of the administration and teaching faculty. Claudia stated that the superintendent had said to them that "whenever you have a complaint about someone you should write and, if appropriate, I would reprimand them." Claudia went on to explain that the superintendent had then added that they would not be told about any action that might be taken, as he felt it was something that should be private between him and his staff. The meeting ended there; again, there was no resolution.

On February 3, 1989, a letter was written to Claudia and Pat by one of the special education consultants from the State Department of Education whom they had met after the referral meeting that took place just after Patrick had entered second grade. The representative had spoken to Pat earlier that day, and Pat had told him that Patrick was making good progress in his education at home. The representative stated:

I was pleased to learn that Patrick is progressing so well in his home education program. As I mentioned, I am attempting to close some outstanding files, including the complaint you submitted relative to the school district's not implementing a mediated agreement. . . .

. . . In Patrick's case, the district opted not to pursue a classification of educationally handicapped, and Patrick is now being given a home education program. Since he is not identified as educationally handicapped, the regulations (STANDARDS) relative to special education do not apply. . . .

Because of these circumstances, the file of the complaint you submitted will be closed effective this date. . . .

Ruled on and disposed of, effective as of that date, Patrick was officially disenfranchised, his right to a public education taken away. His learning was denied, not by any one individual, however unprofessional his behavior may have been, not by the school system, however ill-equipped it may be to support and enhance his learning, and not by the state department of education, even though it may be criticized for ethical indifference for not investigating the mistreatment or even abuse of Patrick and, by extension, his family. Instead, it would

appear to be more accurate to state that Patrick's education has been
denied by the collusive logic that binds together all of these visible and
invisible sociopolitical educational contexts—the individuals and the
institutions—that have had an impact upon his ability to read and write
in school. The myth of a learning disability was socially constructed
by lawmakers, administrators, and teachers and by those who, through
the production of inappropriate educational programs and tests, make
education such a commercial enterprise. Within these contexts, no value
has been placed upon Patrick's ability to create stories, or upon the
risks he takes as he reinvents written language. Patrick the child is not
important. It does not matter what he thinks or what he feels. The goal
of the system is to make him fit, to be the same, to conform to the
pattern, and to learn one way, but never *his* way.

In writing and in reading about Patrick, our task is to make his life
count, to show that it is worth something, to make others see that what
is happening to Patrick can and does happen to many children, not
because they cannot learn but because the system is set up to stop them
learning. When Patrick fails, we all fail. His difficulties are our
difficulties, for we are a part of the sociopolitical contexts that have
falsified his life. What hurts Claudia and Pat the most is that they know
that all this does not have to be. Patrick's early years in school could
have been so different. They know that in a school in which
administrators and teachers support the early literacy behaviors of
children through providing them with opportunities to read books and
write stories, Patrick would have thrived. Indeed, they have advocated
that children be given such opportunities. In 1989 they attended a
number of seminars given to provide teachers with the training that they
need to develop biographic literacy profiles of the children in their
classes, similar to the one I developed for Patrick in the summer before
he entered second grade. Thus, while Claudia and Pat have not been
able to change the system for Patrick, Patrick is changing the system for
literally thousands of children. At one such meeting, Pat stood up at
the end of the day. "They're just kids," he said. "I know it is
sometimes difficult, but they're kids, just kids." Pat spoke for a few
minutes, and many of the teachers were moved, for as he spoke he
touched their lives in a very personal way. What Pat tried to say, James
Agee once tried to write. In his book *Let Us Now Praise Famous
Men*, Agee expressed it this way:

> But let what I have tried to suggest amount to this alone: that not only
> within present reach of human intelligence, but even within reach of mine
> as it stands today, it would be possible that young human beings should rise
> onto their feet a great deal less dreadfully crippled than they are, a great
> deal more nearly capable of living well, a great deal more aware, each of

them, of their own dignity in existence, a great deal better qualified, each within his limits, to live and to take part toward the creation of a world in which good living will be possible without guilt toward every neighbor: and that teaching at present, such as it is, is almost entirely either irrelevant to these possibilities or destructive of them, and is, indeed, all but entirely unsuccessful even within its own "scales" of "value." (p. 294)

Postscript:
Patrick's Universe

In May 1990, Claudia drove to the school district's administration office and asked to see the documentation in Patrick's files. The secretary looked for the files but was unable to find them. She told Claudia that they were probably at the school. Claudia left the building and drove to the elementary school that Patrick had attended. There she was met by his first-grade teacher, who showed her a file in which there was just one sheet of paper, the referral that had been written at the beginning of Patrick's second-grade year. Several days later Claudia made another visit to the administration building and was told that a letter had been written to her regarding her son's files. About a week later, Claudia received a letter from the director of special education in which he stated, "My secretary made me aware that you came to my office yesterday wishing to review your son's school records. There has been no change since you last reviewed these records." Claudia and Pat received another letter from the director of special education the following week, together with the "procedures and guidelines that are required of both parents and school personnel relative to student records." The letter directed their attention to the section that focused upon "procedure to inspect education records." The procedure included a requirement for "a written request which identifies as precisely as possible the records [*sic*] or records he or she wishes to inspect." Claudia wrote a letter to the superintendent of schools requesting an appointment to view all of the school system's documentation pertaining to Patrick. Eventually, arrangements were made for her to view the files.

On her next visit to the school system's administrative offices Claudia was given five files to review. There were three documents in the files that Claudia had not seen before. The first was a memo from Patrick's second grade teacher grading Patrick in phonics, spelling, handwriting, and oral reading. The second document was a letter written by the school district's lawyer. The third was an individualized education plan that had been written for Patrick before he entered first grade.

The letter that the lawyer had written was addressed to the director of the special education mediation program at the state Department of Education. It was another salvo in the dispute over mediation. The lawyer wrote:

> I believe my letter did not request that mediators monitor the actions by school districts during mediation. It is my understanding that during the mediation process you personally advised members of the school's mediation team that in order to reach a mediated agreement, the Department would be willing to allow the requirements contained in the state standards to not be followed. It is disingenuous to state that the school district, of its volition, entered into a flawed mediation agreement. . . . The assertion that it is not the responsibility of the mediators to proofread agreements is intriguing. I had assumed that the reason mediators are given training concerning the special education regulations was to enable them to guide the mediation process to avoid the problems which occurred in this case. In addition to school districts, surely someone, somewhere, at sometime must be responsible for something.

Claudia and Pat had never considered the possibility that an agreement had been made between the state and the school district regarding the mediation agreement. If the lawyer's letter was more than just a smoke screen, what would have happened if there actually had been a due process hearing? Would someone have been "responsible for something" or would the collusive logic binding together the individuals in their institutions have resulted in an overt collusion to code Patrick? Worried about this possibility, Claudia drove to the state capital and visited the office of the director of the mediation program at the Department of Education. The director told her that she had no knowledge of the letter that Claudia had found in Patrick's file. Claudia subsequently sent her a copy of the letter and asked her to respond to the allegations that it contains. So far Claudia has received no reply.

The individualized education plan that Claudia found in 1990 was written for the 1986–87 school year, yet Claudia had never seen it on any of the earlier occasions when she had reviewed the files in preparation for the due process hearing. Claudia and Pat found the plan deeply disturbing, and they were both angry to see that their names were included in the list of plan "developers." The plan was based on the occupational therapy evaluations that were made when Patrick was in kindergarten, and it focused upon what were described as his slightly negative reactions to being touched unexpectedly, his inadequate bilateral coordination skills, his slightly delayed equilibrium reactions, and his inability to stabilize his body in an antigravity position. There were four goals and several short-term objectives for each goal:

1. *Annual Goal*: To enhance and develop tactile perception to allow for increased motor skills.

   Short Term Objective

   a. Patrick will hold his pencil in a neat pincer grasp 100% of the time.
   b. Patrick will demonstrate age-appropriate fine motor skills in copying 10 geometric shapes.
   c. Patrick will be able to accept 5 tactile stimuli with vision occluded without adverse reactions.
   d. Patrick will consistently use the right hand for all skilled tasks.

2. *Annual Goal*: To increase ocular-motor or visual-motor control.

   Short Term Objective

   a. Patrick will track smoothly with his eyes in all directions without irregular or jerky movements 100% of time tested.
   b. Patrick will be able to visually follow a moving object for a distance of 3 feet horizontally and vertically.
   c. Patrick will be able to visually fixate even when engaged in a motor activity such as ball playing 50% [of the] time.

3. *Annual Goal*: To increase postural and bilateral coordination.

   Short Term Goal

   a. Patrick will learn 3 new bilateral coordination skills and perform these age-appropriate skills.
   b. Patrick will be able to stabilize his body in the sitting position on a T stool for 10 sec. without falling off.
   c. Patrick will be able to stand on one foot for 5 sec. with eyes open and closed.
   d. Patrick will be able to hop, skip and jump without any hesitation or irregularity in his steps.
   e. Patrick will be able to use either hand on both sides of his body without shifting or turning 75% of the time observed.

4. *Annual Goal*: To improve expressive language skills.

   Short Term Objective

   a. Patrick will describe a naked item giving at least five characteristics in terms of shape, size, color, use and location with 80% accuracy.

b. Patrick will follow two level directions given one presentation with 90% accuracy for four consecutive sessions.
c. Given part of a story, Patrick will complete the story, providing a logical ending/completion with 80% accuracy for four consecutive sessions.
d. Patrick will sequence five picture cards in correct order and state what is occurring in each picture with 90% accuracy for four consecutive sessions.

Claudia and Pat read the document many times. Claudia said that the plan "brought it all back" but left her with more questions. Why were they never told about the plan? Was the plan used when Patrick was pulled out of his classroom for occupational therapy in the fall of his first-grade year? If enacted on a long-term basis, what impact would this individualized form of instruction have had upon his ability to learn? Would he still have produced his book on the Solar System? Would he have gone on to study the universe?

In the introduction to his book on the universe, Patrick writes:

I was fasinated with the stuff you could learn about the solar system so I wrote a book and called it The Solar System. Then I got interested in the Universe and decided to write another book. This book is called Our Universe. I have also made a mobile of the solar system. I like all the planet's because each one is different. I was most fasinated by black holes, the solar system, sunspots and the Universe.

Patrick spent four months researching the universe, using adult texts as well as children's books. Much of his time was spent in cross-referencing information, going from one book to another as he tried to understand the complexities of the vastness of space. Claudia and Pat worked with him, learning as they went along. Some days were spent just talking about super giants and black holes. Patrick made detailed notes, creating invented spelling of words that were unfamiliar to him. Notes were edited, often expanded, and frequently modified. Eventually the book was finished, and it includes chapters on sunspots, comets, the planets, black holes and nebulae. Patrick describes Jupiter as "the sun that never grew up," and he explains that "sunspots hold gas in then the gas pressure increases and explodes causeing solar flares and prominences." In the chapter on galaxies Patrick writes:

Some scientists think blackholes go into another dimention. Anything that goes near them gets sucked in. There are some in the Milky Way galaxy and some in other galaxies. Some are bigger than others. I think some blackholes contain alot of gases and have alot of force, light goes in and doesn't come out. That means if man ever went in one he wouldn't come out—he might die, or he might find another dimention with people just like us or a differant kind of people (it is not likely because man hasn't even gotton to mars but Voyager 1 or 2 could get sucked in one). It is all theory!

Sitting at the kitchen table, Patrick talked to me about his study of the universe. We looked through the book and discussed the way in which he had constructed the glossary. Patrick talked about looking the words up in a dictionary. "Some of them I didn't really understand and stuff like that, or I'd look them up in my space project."

"So you'd go back into your text, right?"

"Yes."

"Back into what you'd written?"

"Yes."

I asked Patrick, "How many different ways can you find information?"

He paused for a second and then said, "Books. Books. Really books."

"Lots and lots of reference books."

"Mmm. Books, magazines, and sometimes my own ideas. Sometimes what I think."

We continued talking and Patrick said, "Another thing I wanted to show you—" he looked through some papers—"not this—this." It was the beginnings of a bar graph.

"Wow. This is 'absolute magnitude,' " I said, reading the vertical axis.

Patrick added, "That's a bracket," as we both read "Brightness," the word inside the bracket to explain absolute magnitude.

"What does that mean?" I asked. It was a real question.

"Absolute magnitude, brightness?" Patrick repeated, eyes wide, looking at me as he always did when I asked questions that showed how little I know about the universe. "It's the absolute brightness," Patrick explained.

"Of?" I persisted.

"Of the star," he added, as if it was self-explanatory.

He went on to explain the graph. The horizontal axis measured the temperature of stars in kelvins, so Patrick's graph would show the relationship between the surface temperature of a star and its brightness. He went on to talk about the positioning of various stars on the graph. "And then I need to draw say a blue sun here, a little blue sun here and a big blue sun here, a big red sun like that, brown. Stuff like that. What I need to do is get back, you know, that *Our Universe* book in the library?"

"Yes."

"I need to get that one back in order to do this." Patrick talked about getting the book, and then I attempted an explanation of his graph.

"So this is the absolute magnitude, which is brightness of the stars."

"Yes."

"And here you have the temperature—" Patrick joined in and together we said, "in kelvins."

Patrick explained, "That's hotter than the temperature. It's like measuring in degrees but a little bit hotter than degrees. See this is kelvins, thirty thousand degrees, twenty thousand degrees, ten thousand, seven thousand, five thousand, until one thousand."

Struggling with the idea, I said, "So if you had a very, very bright star?"

"Say, a very, very bright star like that red one here?"

"Mmm-hmm."

"That would probably only go to about two thousand degrees."

"Two thousand kelvins? What kind of star would be thirty thousand kelvins?"

"The little blue one," Patrick pointed to the place on the graph where he would position the blue star. "Right about here would be thirty thousand degrees, and our sun would be right about here."

"In the middle of all this."

"Probably be about eight thousand degrees."

"I'm looking forward to seeing this. I think this is great. It's really complicated."

"And a red dwarf and a brown dwarf would be right about here and here. So they'd be as hot, if we had them as like our sun, they'd be as hot as that red super giant way up here."

"Mmm-hmm. So the blue star—" I began.

"The blue giants," Patrick corrected.

"The blue giants—"

"Would be the hottest," Patrick added, helping me out.

"But are they very bright?"

"They're not that bright. They wouldn't—if we had them for our star, just consider it as a star like our star—we wouldn't get as much heat."

"Even though they are very hot?"

"Even—yes," Patrick said.

"Why is that?"

"Because the brightness," Patrick began, "the brightness doesn't—" Patrick tried to explain.

After a few moments I interrupted: "Say it again. I'm lost."

"Well . . ."

"You're doing all right. It's just that I don't know this stuff."

"Well the hotness—the hotness of the star—is thirty thousand degrees. It's how bright it is and the blue super giant is not that bright."

"Isn't that interesting because you'd think that if it was very, very hot then it would be very, very bright, and it doesn't work that way, does it?"

"No. Say the red super giant, now if we had that for our sun then we'd have more heat."

This conversation continued, as had many other conversations, with Patrick explaining theories and developing hypotheses about the "what if's" of our existence here on Earth. Thousands of years from now, will our sun expand and eventually implode? Will Earth, along with Jupiter, Saturn, and Mars, be pulled into the black hole created by the massive implosion? Will a new universe be created? Will there be life on another planet as there is life right now on Earth? Is it possible for us to really know what will happen? Perhaps the best we will ever do is imagine. Contemplating such questions, Patrick wrote in the introduction to his book on the universe, "There is so much to know in so little time." Let us hope that eventually the institution we call school will make time for Patrick, recognize his learning, and praise him for becoming a literate child.

Appendix 1

Tests That Patrick Has Taken in Two and a Half Years of Schooling (K–2)

In preparation for the due process hearing, Claudia and I coded all the documents in Patrick's files that we had managed to obtain. Kindergarten is designated with a K; first grade, 1; and second grade, 2. The documents were also numbered in chronological order. The tests appear in the order in which they were given. The gaps in the numbers below indicate that what came between were letters, reports, and referrals not included here.

Document K-1   *Pre-Kindergarten Developmental Screening*
Subtests:

      Imitate
      Copies
      Traces
      Colors with Lines
      Copies First Name
      Draw a Person
      Build a Tower of Blocks
      Cut
      Running
      Jumping
      Hopping
      Kicking
      Balance Board
      Standing
      Walking
      Stairs and Climbing
      Catching

Rolling and Throwing
Ball Bouncing
Rhythm
Wheel Toys

Hearing
Vision
Color Testing
Gross Motor Development
Fine Motor Development
Speech

Document K-2   *Stanford Early School Achievement Test* (Fall)
Subtests:

The Environment: Social Studies and Science
Math
Letters and Sounds
Aural Comprehension

Document K-10   *Gesell Developmental Evaluation*
Subtests:

Initial Interview
Cubes
Pencil and Paper
   Name
   Copy Forms
   Organization
   Numerals
Incomplete Man
Visual I (matching)
Right-Left
   Single Commands
   Double Commands
Visual III (memory)
Animals
Interests
Tree
Teething
Math Concepts

Document K-12   Occupational Therapy Evaluation
                  Southern California Sensory Integration Tests
                  Subtests: Visual Form and Space Perception

   Space Visualization
   Figure-ground Perception
   Position in Space
   Design Copying

  Subtests: Tactile-Motor Perception

   Kinesthesia
   Manual Form Perception
   Finger Identification
   Graphesthesia
   Localization of Tactile Stimuli
   Double Tactile Stimuli

  Postural and Bilateral Coordination (Listed as
  "skills" not subtests)
   Ocular-Motor Control
   Rapid Forearm Movements
   Postural Insecurity
   Equilibrium Reactions
   Anti-gravity Positions
   Hopping, Skipping, Jumping
   Ball Handling Skills
   Crossing the Midline

  Goodenough Draw-a-Person Test

  Standford Early School Achievement Test (Spring)
  Subtests:

   The Environment: Social Studies and Science
   Math
   Letters and Sounds
   Aural Comprehension

Document K-17   *Oral Motor Examination*

  Clinical Evaluation of Language Functions
  Subtests:

   Processing Word and Sentence Structure
   Word Classes
   Relationships and Ambiguities

Oral Directions
Linguistic Concepts
Spoken Paragraphs
Word Series
Word Associations
Model Sentences
Confrontation Naming
Formulated Sentences

Expressive One-Word Picture Vocabulary Test

Document K-18 *Murphy-Durrell Reading Readiness Analysis*
Subtests:
Phonemes Part I
Phonemes Part II
Letter Names Part I
Letter Names Part II
Learning Rate

Document K-20 *Gesell School Readiness Test*
Subtests:
Cube Test
Initial Interview
Copy Forms
Pencil and Paper
Incomplete Man
Visual I
Visual III
Animals
Interests
Teeth

Document K-23 *Occupational Therapy Re-Evaluation*
Tests:
Kinesthesia
Manual Form Perception
Finger Identification
Graphesthesia
Localization of Tactile Stimuli
Double Tactile Stimuli

Document 1-25   *California Achievement Test (E-11)*
Subtests:

Vocabulary
Categories/Words
Definitions/Words
Synonyms
Words in Context

Comprehension
Sentence Meaning
Passage Details
Stated Main Idea
Character Analysis
Interpreting Events

Language Expression
Nouns
Verbs
Adjectives, Adverbs
Sentence Formation

Math Computation
Add Whole Numbers
Subtract Whole Numbers

Math Concepts and Application
Numeration
Problem Solving
Measurement
Geometry

Word Analysis
Single Consonant/Oral
Consonant Cluster, Digraph/Oral
Long Vowels/Oral
Short Vowels/Oral
Sight Words/Oral

Cognitive Skills Index
Sequencing
Analogies
Memory
Verbal Reasoning

Document 1-35   *KeyMath: Diagnostic Arithmetic Test*
                 Subtests:

        Numeration
        Numerical Reasoning
        Geometry and Symbols
        Addition
        Subtraction
        Mental Computation
        Money
        Measurement
        Time
        Fractions

Document 2-45   *California Achievement Test (E-11)*
                 Subtests:

        Vocabulary
           Categories/Words
           Definitions/Words
           Synonyms
           Words in Context

        Comprehension
           Sentence Meaning
           Passage Details
           Stated Main Idea
           Character Analysis
           Interpreting Events

        Language Expression
           Nouns
           Verbs
           Adjectives, Adverbs
           Sentence Formation

        Math Computation
           Add Whole Numbers
           Subtract Whole Numbers

        Math Concepts and Application
           Numeration
           Problem Solving
           Measurement
           Geometry

Word Analysis
  Single Consonant/Oral
  Consonant Cluster, Digraph/Oral
  Long Vowels/Oral
  Short Vowels/Oral
  Sight Words/Oral

Cognitive Skills Index
  Sequencing
  Analogies
  Memory
  Verbal Reasoning

Document 2-57   *Wechsler Intelligence Scale for Children-Revised*
Verbal Tests:

  Information
  Similarities
  Arithmetic
  Vocabulary
  Comprehension
  Digit Span

Performance Tests:

  Picture Completion
  Picture Arrangement
  Block Design
  Object Assembly
  Coding

Tests Administered by a Clinical Psychologist (September of First Grade)

1. *Wechsler Intelligence Scale for Children—Revised*
Verbal Tests:

  Information
  Similarities
  Arithmetic
  Vocabulary
  Comprehension
  Digit Span

Performance Tests:
  Picture Completion
  Picture Arrangement
  Block Design
  Object Assembly
  Coding

2. *Clinical Evaluation of Language Function*
     Subtests:
       Processing Word and Sentence Structure
       Word Classes
       Relationships and Ambiguities
       Oral Directions
       Linguistic Concepts
       Spoken Paragraphs
       Word Series
       Word Associations
       Model Sentences
       Confrontation Naming
       Formulated Sentences

3. *Beery VMI*

4. *Wide Range Achievement Test*

5. *Personality Inventory for Children*

6. *Peabody Picture Vocabulary*

7. *Lateral Dominance Examination*

8. *Asphasia Screen*

9. *Sensory and Perceptual Exam*

10. *Trail Tests*

11. *ABC Test for Ocular Dominance*

Further testing has been advocated by the school system.

Appendix 2

Contradictory Statements Written About Patrick That Create an Invalid and Misleading Record of Learning Disabilities

Document K-4	"rather clumsy pencil grip"
Document K-9	"pencil grip appeared fine"
Document K-9	"Appeared to take some of his ideas from other students"
Document K-16	"Does not take cues from other students and teacher in class. Immaturity?"
Document K-10	"inner time table of maturation . . . criteria for placement"
Document K-12	"difficulties . . . are not necessarily going to go away with maturity"
Document K-11	"I've included copies of the Visual Memory subtest. He really did do well in it . . . (like an older child!)"
Document K-20	"It should perhaps be noted that the two areas where Patrick had the most difficulty (steps 6 and 10 of the Cube Test of Visual 3) both require visual memory."
Document K-12	"Ocular-motor control—some irregularity"
Document K-12a	(Opticians Report) "No ocular dysfunction"

| Document K-23 | "Patrick was able to stay on task much more effectively during the administration of these tests." |
| Document K-23 | "At times, Patrick's attention for the task was at risk and I had to bring him back to task." |

| Document 1-35 | "Above grade level . . . numerical 2.8 numerical reasoning 2.6 grade level" |
| Document 1-36 | "In math he is below the group." |

| Document 1-38 | "the single characteristic that distinguishes him from the students is his difficulty working independently" |
| Document 1-39 | "works independently S + " |

| Document K-20 | "Patrick was very co-operative and worked carefully and thoughtfully throughout the test. He was quiet and sat unusually still exhibiting no overflow behavior." |
| Document 2-57 | "He gave his answers impulsively instead of reflecting on them. His answers were practically out before the questions ended." |

| Document K-10 | "Patrick works with a definite sense of purpose. He does his best and appears unconcerned with his errors." |
| Document 2-57 | "Patrick also seems to have a driven quality about him. It is as if too much were riding on his answers—perhaps his self-esteem or the approval of others." |

Appendix 3

Myth-Making Statements

Recorded in Patrick's

School Folders

Document K-1	"possible perceptual problems" "should be watched"
Document K-4	"rather clumsy pencil grip" "internal organization seems a problem" "is impulsive" "had trouble with auditory sequencing activity"
Document K-4a	"may need to improve his gross motor skills"
Document K-5	"difficulty following directions"
Document K-9	"interaction with other students almost sarcastic" "seemed easily distracted by other students"
Document K-10	"undifferentiated motor responses" "vertical and horizontal reversals" "does not cross over" "questionable visual perception" "young perceptual motor patterns" "appears to have to exclude alternatives"
Document K-11	"unable to assume various anti-gravity postures without great exertion" "hopping, jumping, skipping . . . slightly below grade level"

Document K-15   "very hesitant, doesn't take risks or sequence
                       activities very well"

Document K-19   "needs the extra time of another year in kinder-
                       garten"

Document K-22   "I cannot vouch for what happens to the sound
                       once it reaches his brain"

Document K-23   "some resistance to being touched and positioned
                       with eyes closed"

Document K-23   "include activities to increase tactile perception"

Document 1-28   "looks baffled"

Document 1-29   "the beginning of frustration and school avoidance"
                       "kids were not picking on him until he made
                       himself different"

Document 1-30   "Patrick tries hard to please"
                       "It is important that we complete his testing"

Document 1-32   "continues to have difficulty in consistently crossing
                       his midline"

Document 1-36   "First grade teacher [name in document] saw at
                       beginning of year a happy bouncy boy—now un-
                       happy"

Document 2-42   "lack of phonetic analysis skills"
                       "cannot read phonetically which further leads that he
                       cannot comprehend what he is reading"
                       "lack of spatial relationships between letters and
                       words"

Document 2-48   "Patrick will go through the mechanics but seems to
                       lack comprehension"
                       "When Patrick looks at a word he seems not to
                       interpret the way others do"

Document 2-59   "continues, however, to struggle with words or
                       sentences in isolation"

Bibliography

Agee, James, and Walker Evans. 1941. *Let Us Now Praise Famous Men.* Boston: Houghton Mifflin.

Anderson, R. C.; E. H. Heibert; J. A. Scott; and I. A. G. Wilkinson. 1985. *Becoming a Nation of Readers: The Report of the Commission on Reading.* Washington, D.C.: The National Institute of Education.

Coles, Gerald S. 1978. "The Learning-Disabilities Test Battery: Empirical and Social Issues." *Harvard Educational Review* 48: 313–40.

―――. 1987. *The Learning Mystique: A Critical Look at "Learning Disabilities."* New York: Pantheon Books.

Elkind, David. 1981. *The Hurried Child: Growing Up Too Fast Too Soon.* Reading, MA: Addison-Wesley.

Gartner, Alan, and Dorothy Kerzner Lipsky. 1987. "Beyond Special Education: Toward a Quality System for All Students." *Harvard Educational Review* 57: 367–95.

Goodman, Kenneth S. 1988. "Look What They've Done to Judy Blume!: The 'Basalization' of Children's Literature." *The New Advocate* 1 (1): 29–41.

Goodman, Kenneth S., Patrick Shannon, Yvonne S. Freeman, and Sharon Murphy. 1988. *Report Card on Basal Readers.* Katonah, NY: Richard C. Owens Publishers, Inc.

Granger, Lori, and Bill Granger. 1986. *The Magic Feather: The Truth About Special Education.* New York: E. P. Dutton.

Greene, Maxine. 1978. *Landscapes of Learning.* New York and London: Teachers College Press.

Lieberman, Laurence M. 1984. *Preventing Special Education... For Those Who Don't Need It.* Weston, MA: Nob Hill Press, Inc.

Martin, Anne. 1988. "Teachers and Teaching. Screening, Early Intervention, and Remediation: Obscuring Children's Potential." *Harvard Educational Review* 58: 488–501.

Mehan, Hugh. 1984. "Institutional Decision Making." In Barbara Rogoff and Jean Lave, eds., *Everyday Cognition: Its Development in Social Context*. Cambridge: Harvard University Press.

Mehan, Hugh; Alma Hertweck; and J. Lee Meihls. 1986. *Handicapping the Handicapped: Decision Making in Students' Educational Careers*. Stanford, CA: Stanford University Press.

Poplin, Mary S. 1988. "The Reductionistic Fallacy in Learning Disabilities: Replicating the Past by Reducing the Present." *Journal of Learning Disabilities* 21: 389–400.

Rose, Mike. 1989. *Lives on the Boundary: The Struggles and Achievements of America's Underprepared*. New York: The Free Press.

Sapon-Shevin, Mara. 1989. "Mild Disabilities: In and Out of Special Education." In Douglas Biklen, Dianne L. Ferguson, and Alison Ford (eds.), *Schooling and Disability: Eighty-eighth Yearbook of the National Society for the Study of Education*. Part II. Chicago: The University of Chicago Press.

Taylor, Denny. 1988. "Ethnographic Educational Evaluation for Children, Families, and School." *Theory into Practice* 27 (1): 67–76.

———. 1990. "Teaching Without Testing." *English Education* 22 (1): 4–74.

———. In press. "From the Child's Point of View: Alternate Approaches to Assessment." To be published in Jessie Roderick and Judith L. Green (eds.), *Developing Context-Responsive Approaches to Assessment*. Urbana, IL: National Council of Research in English.

Taylor, Denny, and Catherine Dorsey-Gaines. 1988. *Growing Up Literate: Learning from Inner-City Families*. Portsmouth, N.H.: Heinemann.